THIN BLUE FAULT LINE—
POLICING AMERICA

ABOUT THE AUTHORS

John C. Franklin's career in policing has spanned over 34 years. He is a 28-year veteran of the Chicago Police Department where he rose from patrol officer to commander before retiring in 2010. Since retiring from the Chicago Police Department he served as chief of the Dolton, IL Police Department in suburban Chicago and also as the Chief of Police, Jacksonville Arkansas. He also served as an adjunct professor of criminal justice at a Midwestern college. Between classes he mentored students seeking careers in law enforcement.

Franklin holds a bachelor's degree in media communications and a master's degree in criminal/social justice. He is a graduate of the Chicago Police Executive Development Program and the Northwestern University's Center for Public Safety/School of Police Staff and Command. He has co-authored two articles for PoliceOne.com with John F. Hein.

John F. Hein is a former university adjunct professor of criminal justice and a retired executive of the former U.S. Customs Service. Hein served 35 years in civilian and military security and law enforcement agencies. He began his civilian law enforcement career as a deputy sheriff in Joliet, Illinois. He spent 27 years as a special agent/criminal investigator in three federal agencies in Chicago, Miami, New York City and Washington, DC. During his career he also served as an active duty special agent with U.S. Army Military Intelligence, conducted port security duties with the U.S. Coast Guard Reserve and spent 23 years in the U.S. Air Force Reserve as a special agent with the Air Force Office of Special Investigations. He retired from the U.S. Customs Service when activated by the U.S. Air Force after the September 11, 2001, attacks.

Hein is a member of ASIS International, an association of security professionals, and is a Certified Protection Professional (CPP). He holds a bachelor's degree in Business Administration and a Master's Degree in Public Service. He is a graduate of the Federal Executive Institute, Charlottesville, VA.

He is the author of *Inside Internal Affairs: An In-Depth Look at the People, Process and Politics,* published by Looseleaf Law Publications, Inc. He has authored numerous articles published by PoliceOne.com and FedSmith.com.

THIN BLUE FAULT LINE— POLICING AMERICA

A 21st Century Challenge of Compromise

By

JOHN C. FRANKLIN

and

JOHN F. HEIN, CPP

CHARLES C THOMAS • PUBLISHER, LTD.
Springfield • Illinois • U.S.A.

Published and Distributed Throughout the World by

CHARLES C THOMAS • PUBLISHER, LTD.
2600 South First Street
Springfield, Illinois 62704

© 2021 by CHARLES C THOMAS • PUBLISHER, LTD.

ISBN 978-0-398-09354-9 (paper)
ISBN 978-0-398-09355-6 (ebook)

Library of Congress Catalog Card Number: LCCN 2020052957 (print)
LCCN 2020052958 (ebook)

With THOMAS BOOKS *careful attention is given to all details of manufacturing
and design. It is the Publisher's desire to present books that are satisfactory as to their
physical qualities and artistic possibilities and appropriate for their particular use.*
THOMAS BOOKS *will be true to those laws of quality that assure a good name
and good will.*

*Printed in the United States of America
MM-C-1*

Library of Congress Cataloging-in-Publication Data

Names: Franklin, John C. (Chief of police), author. | Hein, John F.,
author.
Title: Thin blue fault line--policing America : a 21st century challenge of
compromise/ by John C. Franklin and John F. Hein.
Description: Springfield, Illinois : Charles C Thomas, Publisher, Ltd.,
[2021] | Includes bibliographical references and index.
Identifiers: LCCN 2020052957 (print) | LCCN 2020052958 (ebook) | ISBN
9780398093549 (paperback) | ISSN 9780398093556 (ebook)
Subjects: LCSH: Police--United States. | Police-community relations--United
States. | Racial profiling in law enforcement--United States. | African
Americans--Violence against. | United States--Race relations.
Classification: LCC HV8141 .F66 2021 (print) | LCC HV8141 (ebook) | DDC
363.2/30973--dc23
LC record available at https://lccn.loc.gov/2020052957
LC ebook record available at https://lccn.loc.gov/2020052958

PREFACE

The authors of this work come from similar but diverse backgrounds. They share similar views and have collaborated to open a discussion and urge action to save lives. They did not write this book because of attacks on police officers, but because of overzealous actions by police officers to shoot black men.

John C. Franklin, a black man, was raised on the south side of Chicago in a strong, religious, middle-class family with a desire for a law enforcement career at an early age. He became a police officer in 1982 and rose to an executive management position before retiring in 2010. He has both an undergraduate and graduate degree. He taught college level courses as an adjunct professor and relishes mentoring motivated students and up-and-coming police officers.

John F. Hein, a white man, was raised on the south side of Chicago in a strong, religious, middle-class family with a desire for a law enforcement career at an early age. He became a deputy sheriff in 1973, and a federal law enforcement officer in 1974. He rose to an executive management position before retiring in 2001, when recalled to active duty as a military reservist after the 9/11 attacks. He has both an undergraduate and graduate degree. Hein taught college level courses as an adjunct professor and still enjoys mentoring motivated individuals.

It is obvious to the authors many police officers do not understand expectations, sensitivities and demands of 21st century citizens. New century officers must understand he or she must follow a code of ethics and offer justice and fair treatment to all citizens, while also understanding that segments of the public oftentimes feel no restraint and are more than willing to show disrespect and a defiance to authority.

Franklin and Hein have witnessed firsthand difficulties experienced in some black communities. They use their knowledge to analyze and discuss the interactions between American policing, a sub-culture of the black community and the BLM movement. Many ills in some black communities are not adequately addressed and black on black crime continues at an alarming rate. Disputed blue on black shootings do not seem to be subsiding and without efforts from the black community the deadly turmoil between two diverse cultures will continue.

Problems exist in some black communities not only because of racism and inherent discrimination, but because one would not dare criticize certain aspects of black culture in an overall effort to effectively deal with historic and deeply rooted problems. These problems, like absentee fathers and violence in schools, continue to plague many black communities because to violate political correctness would only intensify the resistance to criticism shown by black pundits.

The authors hope their assessment will be viewed as constructive and that it instigates action that continues to improve American policing and begins to expand the horizon of a sub-culture that seems to disrespect itself. The authors do understand, however, their views are controversial and may not be accepted or understood by many even though we have cited many sources of support to present our perspective. We further understand this work may be discounted by some because it is peppered with our personal anecdotes, but we have witnessed what we discuss, we experienced it and discussed it with many others as it happened.

INTRODUCTION

We may anger many because the following contents are controversial. We tell it like we see it and we are not politically correct when we say it. We focus on the police and on how bias, attitudes, strategy and tactics sometimes cause intense citizen responses through public statements, outbursts and demonstrations. We discuss the causation of hostility by people of color; it starts with police actions. We examine the creation of the Black Lives Matter (BLM) movement; it was created because of a pervasive opinion that black men were being killed at an alarming rate by mostly white police officers under controversial circumstances. We explain the movement's contentious relationship with American policing; inflamed by the police. We debate the successes of the BLM movement; unconsciously given strength by the police. We reveal how public demonstrations can become riots because of police militarism. We argue the differences between American policing and the culture of the American black community. We give credit to police leaders for acknowledging these differences and making changes needed to face 21st century challenges. We conclude our discussion with placing responsibility of compromise on seemingly detached, black leaders and pundits, some in denial, who place the ills of the black community solely on discrimination. But, it all starts with historical policing missteps.

Police strategy is the design and direction of the manner in which American policing enforces laws and maintains the public order. Police tactics is the approach and deployment of the overall strategy. Since there are over 18,000 law enforcement organizations in the United States, each department can have a different strategy or strategies depending upon neighborhood composition, citizen cultures, crime rates, economic factors, travel patterns and various other reasons. Tactics, on the other hand, are usually similar in any department because of human factors, policy, procedures, the U.S. Constitution, federal and state court decisions and American ethical and moral attitudes.

Police and citizen frustration runs high when some police actions violate the U.S. Constitution and rules of right conduct. This same wrong conduct causes a media frenzy because of its ability to fill media space and arouse citizen action. Individual citizens and especially citizen advocacy groups confront elected officials and public servants in bewilderment, questioning a policy, decision or action.

Since the first watchmen were recruited in the colonies, problems with corruption and negligence of duty in policing were encountered and finding men who would take the position seriously was difficult. Students of history know during the 17th and 18th and most of the 19th centuries when law enforcement was, for the most part inadequate, private enforcement by railroad barons, sheriff's posse and vigilantes was common. During this period, law enforcement and punishment were frequently taken into individual hands to avenge a crime without authority of law. It was commonplace that retribution was arbitrary and summarily delivered with limited evidence (Wadman & Allison, 2004).

Starting in the late 19th century many civic minded citizens created committees to recommend ways to improve police services. Many recommendations, if implemented, were short lived because of corruption and political agendas. Early in the 20th century, civil service standards helped improve policing but politics continued to stymie many efforts (Wadman & Allison, 2004).

With the passage of the 18th Amendment by U.S. Congress that prohibited the manufacture, sale and transportation of intoxicating liquor, elected officials and, in tandem, American law enforcement, became so scandalously corrupt that in 1929, President Herbert Hoover created the National Committee on Law Observance and Enforcement. The committee, commonly called the Wickersham Commission, found a broad pattern of police misconduct throughout the country (Walker, 1977).

Throughout much of the 20th century, American law enforcement was a public service, like many others, that was undervalued and underfunded. Although undervalued, some in society did appreciate the worth of a professional criminal justice system. Academics like August Vollmer and O.W. Wilson studied policing and Wilson, periodically, put his management theories into practice as chief of police in Fullerton, California, Wichita, Kansas, and finally as Superintendent of the Chicago Police Department. Academia had additional influence by developing scientific applications that were adopted for criminal justice purposes. The federal government had limited influence on local policing through the first half of the 20th century, but the FBI National Academy was opened in 1935, to standardize and professionalize policing across the country (Federal Bureau of Investigation, n.d.). The FBI also led the use of science in American criminal justice.

The federal government had a much greater impact on American law enforcement during the second half of the 20th century. U.S. Supreme Court decisions helped professionalize policing. For example, Mapp v. Ohio, 367

v. 643 (1961), created the exclusionary rule that prohibits evidence collected in violation of the U.S. Constitution from being used in a court of law; Escobedo v. Illinois, 378 U.S. 478 (1964), extended the right of counsel to not only those charged with a crime, but also to those detained for a crime; and, Miranda v. Arizona, 384 U.S. 436 (1966), that required incriminating statements could only be used at trial if the defendant was aware of his right to counsel and his right against self-incrimination. In addition, federal grants, legislation and consent decrees used to reform police departments have all affected American law enforcement in a beneficial way (Jackman, 2017).

Much of the federal efforts begun and legal challenges made in the 1960s were hastened because of the police response to civil rights demonstrations in the 1950s; employing the thoughtless and unwise use of fire hoses and police dogs. It can also be said these efforts had some impact on department modernization, policy and the legal rules of evidence but a lessor impact on police culture.

In the latter half of the 20th century and entering into the 21st century, as officers became more educated and training more demanding, citizens, too, became more educated and more demanding. Recent history has revealed excellent police service, but at the same time there have been lapses in professional conduct that have caused shock and panic among citizens, certainly citizens of color, resulting in demonstrations pleading for more unbiased, less confrontational and adversarial policing tactics.

We intend to outline the problems of American law enforcement in the 21st century thereby explaining why a broad social segment is critical, demanding and demonstrates against American policing. A number of officers cause the majority to be characterized as corrupt, biased and widely unprofessional. It seems when one officer commits egregious misconduct, one size fits all. Exhibitions are sometimes focused on one or a few officers or one department for questionable actions taken, while others can be comprehensive.

However, a wide number of officers may become verbally defiant when confronted with criticism and may show contempt for detractors. Further controversy is created by the way citizen criticism is presented through confrontations and riots and the responding actions taken by American policing to meet the turmoil. One culture meets another.

The culture of any department can be a subculture of the city or area in which its members serve, but a department can also include numerous cultures exhibited by its officers. A department culture can be one developed over many years created by strong ethical leadership or one created by an uncaring corrupt command structure.

In police culture there is a so-called code of silence, the protection of officers no matter what the situation. The code, while not accepted by all, demands 'I see, speak, and hear no evil.' This code contributes to a detachment with citizens that does not appear to be on the mend. Some officers, leaders and seemingly all union officials deny wrongdoing by officers even when no direct knowledge of the incident is apparent. Citizens, typically people of color, are asking, cajoling, challenging, and demanding more professional police service. In response, police representatives criticized, condemned and faulted those who passed severe judgements. Although unwise police responses to criticism is arguably subsiding, citizen actions that sometimes cause questionable police actions is still prevalent. It seems American policing is alone in efforts to make culture changes. In addition, most recent attempts by police to limit blatant violations of policy, rules of right conduct and the U.S. Constitution have been stymied by the lack of federal funding and coordination. No one has yet to step forward to promote and maintain communications between citizens and the police profession in an efficient and courteous manner. Sporadic attempts have been made but none have had confidence of success. It is difficult to problem solve when all sides do not share the same agenda.

We are hopeful this publication will be a small part of a snowball effect causing more serious discussions and comprehensive attempts to resolve complaints and save lives. Currently, American policing is limited by unilateral change and a political climate where many are talking but few are listening.

This narrative may be of special interest to the critics of American policing and those who condemn unprofessional actions, attitudes and command presence by officers. Others may find interest as more controversy is added as we discuss problems caused by subcultures in society that are confronted by American policing.

American policing in the 21st century seems to be more challenging than ever but a greater challenge must be faced by the black community if any lasting changes are to be sustained.

REFERENCES

Federal Bureau of Investigation. (n.d.). Services. National Academy. https://www.fbi.gov/services/training-academy/national-academy

Jackman, T. (2017). Do federal consent decrees improve local police departments? this study says they might. *The Washington Post.* https://www.washingtonpost.com/news/true-crime/wp/2017/05/24/__trashed/

Wadman, R. C., & Allison, W.T. (2004). *To protect and to serve: A history of police in America.* Pearson Education, 47–51, 67–81.

Walker, S. (1977). *A critical history of police reform: the emergence of professionalism.* Lexington Books, D.C. Health & Co, 25.

ACKNOWLEDGMENTS

There are a number of people we thank for their insight, guidance and constructive criticism. We especially thank the designer of the title page. For all those who assisted us, however, there is no recognition. Concerns for our apparent lack of political correctness resulting in possible repercussions gave us sufficient reason to keep identities confidential. We reluctantly withhold our public acknowledgment of their contributions. In addition, all interviews were conducted in confidentiality, and the names of interviewees are withheld by mutual agreement.

CONTENTS

AUTHORS' NOTE: RACE-NEUTRAL REFERENCE

We suggest that since the beginning of time there have been disputed ideas regarding almost everything. We debated how we would identify the traditional divisions of the human race. Our intent is not to insult, disrespect, offend or provoke. There is little to no controversy calling a member of the Caucasian race as white. However, there may be more than a minor debate on how to describe the Negro race. Over time we have heard many descriptions, such as black, Negro and African American. Since we decided to describe the Caucasian race as white throughout this book, we decided to describe the Negro race as black. We also use the terms, such as: blacks, black culture, black subculture, black men, black leaders and black community. Unless the word black begins a sentence, is indexed, is in a chapter title or sub-heading, or is part of a formal title like Black Lives Matter, the term black is not capitalized.

THIN BLUE FAULT LINE—
POLICING AMERICA

Chapter One

CAUSATION OF HOSTILITY
BY PEOPLE OF COLOR

I look to a day when people will not be judged by the color of their skin, but by the content of the character.

> Dr. Martin Luther King, Jr.

American policing has never had a stellar reputation with minorities. It can be said any minority in history has been abused, belittled, taken advantage of and more. This callousness has caused a hostility by the black community towards American policing. Paraphrasing Dr. Victor E. Kappeler in his article: *A Brief History of Slavery and the Origins of American Policing* (2014), he writes:

> The creation and progress of American policing can be traced to many historically significant attitudes, events and conditions. Slavery and the control of slaves, however, were two of the more menacing features of early American society shaping policing. Some modern police departments started out as slave patrols and Night Watches, both designed to control the behaviors of the slaves. Kappeler goes on to say, "For example, New England settlers appointed Indian Constables to police Native Americans (National Constable Association, 1995), the St. Louis police were founded to protect residents from Native Americans in that frontier city, and many southern police departments began as slave patrols. In 1704, the colony of Carolina developed the nation's first slave patrol. Slave patrols helped to maintain the economic order and to assist the wealthy landowners in recovering and punishing slaves who essentially were considered property." (Kappeler 2014)

Again paraphrasing Dr. Kappeler, he states: a person with white skin could also be discriminated against in early America, but being Caucasian unquestionably made things easier for some minorities to be included in the melting pot of America. Persons with black, red, yellow or brown skin has had greater difficulty in assimilating into the mainstream of American society. Kappeler continues to state: "The additional burden of racism has made that transition for those whose skin is black, brown, red, or yellow more difficult. In no small part because of the tradition of slavery, [b]lacks have long been targets of abuse. The use of patrols to capture runaway slaves was one of the precursors of formal police forces, especially in the South. This disastrous legacy persisted as an element of the police role even after the passage of the Civil Rights Act of 1964. In some cases, police harassment simply meant people of African descent were more likely to be stopped and questioned by the police, while at the other extreme, they have suffered beatings, and even murder, at the hands of [w]hite police. Questions still arise today about the disproportionately high numbers of people of African descent killed, beaten, and arrested by police in major urban cities of America." (Kappeler, 2014)

OLD MAN CROW IS DEAD, BUT HIS SPIRIT IS STILL WITH US

In late 1898, white supremacists overthrew the government of the City of Wilmington, NC, and forced the resignation of elected officials. Reportedly, 60 black citizens were killed and many prominent blacks were expelled from the city. In the late 1890s both the white and black communities shared the authority of government, but some whites believed blacks were becoming too powerful because of the number of public offices held. Because of racial prejudice, the principles of democracy were abandoned by the more powerful white community. A group of elite whites issued what was to be known as the Wilmington Declaration of Independence. The declaration announced "whites had the right to 'end the rule by Negroes,'" because the elites paid the vast majority of property taxes (Crain, 2020).

In time, the supremacists altered state law to suppress the black vote and to deprive the black community of their liberties. In 1896, prior to the subversion there were more than one hundred thousand black voters in the state of North Carolina. By 1906, there were only about six thousand black voters in the state (Crain, 2020).

A political handbook was circulated naming America as "white man's country." White Government Union Clubs were organized whose principles called for "the supremacy of the white race" (Crain, 2020).

By 1899, the state legislature passed a constitutional amendment charging a voter's fee or poll tax and requiring voters to pass a literacy test "unless the father or a grandfather had voted before 1867." The amendment was meant to place a restriction on poor black and white voters, too, in order for elite whites to control government. In addition, the legislature eventually passed Jim Crow laws segregating passenger rail cars, along with toilets, parks, water fountains and even courtroom Bibles (Crain, 2020).

The state of North Carolina is still attempting to suppress the vote as we enter into the third decade of the 21st century. In 2018, the legislature enacted a constitutional amendment that limits voter participation to those who possess state-issued photo identification (Crain, 2020).

According to the Jim Crow Museum of Racist Memorabilia, Jim Crow refers to a caste system which operated primarily in southern and Border States to segregate Black Americans from whites. Beginning in 1877, Jim Crow laws, black codes or etiquettes created a way of life and restricted the liberties of blacks.

The Jim Crow Museum of Racist Memorabilia is located on the campus of Ferris State University, Big Rapids, MI. David Pilgram calls himself a collector of racist garbage. He believes Jim Crow laws are more than a collection of 'whites only' signs, but the imagery and others like it supported the laws and the life they created for blacks. Pilgram does not want the horrors of Jim Crow to be ignored. He believes long before the September 11, 2001, attacks, blacks were well acquainted with terrorism. He found that many students, both black and white, believed he was exaggerating when he showed them his collection and described the awfulness of Jim Crow. The museum collection and others like it depict "all the hurt and harm done to Africans and their American descendants." The museum is a teaching laboratory; using items of intolerance to teach tolerance (Pilgram, 2012).

States that recognized the caste system authorized the placement of Jim Crow 'white only' or 'black only' signs above water fountains, door entrances and exits and other facilities where blacks and whites transited. There were separate hospitals, schools, churches, restrooms and prisons. Visitors of the American Museum of American History in Washington, DC can view a section of a lunch counter from the Woolworth's store in Greensboro, NC.

According to the museum website: "Racial segregation was still legal in the United States on February 1, 1960, when four African American college students sat down at this [pictured on the website] Woolworth counter in Greensboro, North Carolina. Politely asking for service at this "whites only" counter, their request was refused. When asked to leave, they remained in their seats. Their sit-in drew national attention and helped ignite a youth-led movement to challenge inequality throughout the South. Protests such as this led to the passage of the Civil Rights Act of 1964, which finally outlawed racial segregation in public accommodations" (Pilgram, 2012).

Many Christian theologians taught their followers the white race represented the Chosen people and, therefore, many Christians believed God supported racial segregation. Many medical professionals believed blacks were intellectually and culturally inferior to whites. Many politicians gave speeches attesting to the inferiority of blacks and the dangers of integration and mixing races. Many whites believed treating blacks as equals would encourage mixed unions producing interracial children which would destroy America (Pilgram, 2012).

A black man could not shake hands with a white man and even an attempt to offer a hand to a white women risked he be accused of rape. Because of implied intimacy, a black man could not offer to light a cigarette for a white woman. The races were not to eat together, but if they did, a partition would separate the races and whites were to be served first. Blacks could not show affection in public because it would offend whites. Etiquette also held that a white man or woman was never introduced to a black person, a black man or women must be introduced to a white person. Whites never used a courtesy title like 'sir' or ma'am for a black person, but called them by their first name (Pilgram, 2012).

According to the Jim Crow Museum of Racist Memorabilia:

- Oklahoma prohibited blacks and whites from boating together.
- In 1905, Georgia created separate parks for blacks and whites.

- Alabama required all bus and train passenger stations to operate separate waiting rooms and ticket windows for the white and 'colored' races. In 1930, Birmingham, Alabama, prohibited the races to play checkers or dominoes together. Alabama directed that a white nurse could not care for a black man.
- Georgia prohibited 'colored' barbers to care for white girls or women.
- Louisiana maintained separate facilities for blind patients.
- South Carolina made it illegal for a parent or guardian to permanently place a white child in the custody of a 'negro'. North Carolina also directed that the state librarian maintain a separate space for 'colored people who want to read books or periodicals.
- Florida operated separate schools for white and 'negro' children (as did many other southern states).
- Oklahoma deemed it a misdemeanor for anyone to instruct at any school that enrolls members of both the white and 'color' races.
- Georgia directed that anyone licensed to sell beer and wine must sell exclusively to white people or black people, but not to both races in the same room.

The Jim Crow Museum website continues to detail that the criminal justice system supported the caste system. Blacks who had the nerve to violate the system risked their jobs, homes and lives. Public lynching of blacks, and many whites, was not unusual in the 1800s, but by the mid to late 1800s and into the early 1900s blacks became the most frequent victims. There was little to no justice metered when the police, prosecutors, judges, juries and prison officials were all white.

In 1865, the 13th Amendment to the U.S. Constitution ended slavery. In 1868, the 14th Amendment granted U.S. citizenship to all former slaves and guaranteed equal protection under the law. In 1870, the 15th Amendment granted black men the right to vote. However, a key U.S. Supreme Court case, 163 U.S. 537 (1896) [Plessy v Ferguson] stymied civil rights efforts when the court upheld racial segregation laws. The Court created the doctrine: 'separate but equal'. The decision undermined Constitutional protections and legitimized a Jim Crow life for blacks (Pilgram, 2012).

Black men were denied the right to vote by: 1) Grandfather clauses, only allowing blacks to vote whose ancestors voted before the civil war. This denied the vote to all black men, since ancestors of black men were slaves who were property and had no rights or who were freed black men who had no right to vote prior to the passage of the 15th Amendment. 2) Poll taxes, charged only to blacks who could not afford the tax. A Poll tax is a fee levied by a government to raise funds. (Some states used Poll taxes to generate government funding and was not an unusual request.) According to the National Museum of American History website Poll taxes were not begun in southern states until 1890. They were used as a legal way to deny African Americans the right to vote. The Grandfather clause excused some poor whites from paying the fee if their ancestors voted before the civil war. 3) White primaries, only whites could vote in a Democratic primary because only whites could be Democrats. 4) Literacy tests, which only a well-read person could possibly pass (Pilgram, 2012).

The Jim Crow era was between 1877 and the mid-1960s, but some would say it ain't over till it's over.

A DECADE CAUSING CHANGE

Anyone of age in the 1960s will remember a violent confrontation in Birmingham, Alabama, between police and people of color demonstrating for equality. Eugene "Bull' Connor was Commissioner of Public Safety in Birmingham and oversaw the fire and police departments during the time of frequent civil rights demonstrations in numerous southern states. Connor was a hostile and aggressive opponent of civil rights issues and vigorously enforced *legal* segregation. Connor infamously ordered fire hoses and police dogs be used on children demonstrating for equality. As the debacle was broadcast on the nightly news, the nation was outraged. President John Kennedy said, "The civil rights movement should thank God for Bull Connor. He helped it as much as Abraham Lincoln" (Nunnelly, 1991). Issuing the Emancipation Proclamation, a presidential executive order, President Lincoln effectively ended slavery in the United States on January 1, 1863. Bull Connor's aggressive tactics, one hundred years later, brought forth to the American public the ills the civil rights movement was demonstrating against, even the difficulties of traveling while black.

THE ENJOYMENT OF DOMESTIC TRAVEL

Another example of discrimination and hatred by whites and the causation of hostility by blacks is showcased in the 2018 film, Green Book. The film, based on the true experiences of a black pianist and his white escort, chronicle their travel through the 1960s Deep South as the pianist entertains and the escort protects him from white bigotry. The Negro Motorist Green-Book is a traveler's guide, published by a New York City postal worker, from 1936 to 1966. The guide helped "black folks" traverse the dangers and humiliations of the racially segregated South. The book listed gas stations, restaurants, barber shops and hair salons, rooming houses and other businesses black travelers could safely patronize without rejection or harm (Moodie-Mills, 2017).

Another interesting part of the Green Book was the first message written by author Victor Green telling black travelers to be respectable and to act as ambassadors of the black community. "Back then it mattered how you looked. For some if you dressed well you may be treated a little better, not always, but sometimes" (Moodie-Mills, 2017).

On BLACKPAST.org, the *Online Reference Guide to African American History*, one more stinging bit of information was that "African American motorists . . . were warned to avoid sundown towns which required minorities to be outside the city limits before sundown, hence the name." If discovered after dark, some were escorted out of town by the police to fend for themselves (Tunnell, 2014).

CHANGES COULDN'T COME FAST ENOUGH

As the last half of the 20th century continued, so did the insults and abuse directed against minority citizens by police. Some are most infamous:

- Chicago Police Lt. Jon Burge was accused along with others of torture against more than a hundred mostly black suspects in the 1970s, 80s, and 90s to coerce confessions. Under suspicion and investigation for many years, Burge was not fired by the Chicago Police Department until 1993. He was convicted on federal charges in 2010 and sentenced to four-and-a-half-years in a federal penitentiary. Reportedly, the City of Chicago paid many millions of dollars to victims of Burge and his associates (People' Law Office, 2012).

- The disputed beating of Rodney King in March 1991 made King a notorious, internationally known personality following a high-speed police chase. The incident caused a public outcry and renewed concerns of police excessive use of force when dealing with minorities. In April, 1992, the vindication of four officers charged with assault and excessive use of force against King provoked riots in Los Angeles where a number of people were killed and countless were injured (National Public Radio 2017). King appeared on television during the riots and said, "Can't we all just get along?" (Brownson, 2017).

- Brutalization of African Americans continued when Abner Louima was assaulted on August 9, 1997, by New York City Police Officer Justin Volpe. After being arrested in a disturbance, Louima was beaten and sodomized with a broomstick that required a 2-month long hospital stay. Louima was treated for a ruptured colon and bladder. Volpe was convicted of civil rights violations and sentenced to 30-years in prison. One other officer who once believed in the police code of silence served a 5-year sentence for perjury for his attempt to cover-up the incident (Grunlund, 2017).

I did not experience great pain growing up black in the city. I was very fortunate to have matured in a middle-class black family. My parents always told me I was as good and intelligent as anyone else, regardless of what some of my white teachers may have said to me and other black students in the classroom. Even after attending college away from home at Northern Illinois University, I can honestly say that the most racism I ever encountered throughout my life was as a Chicago Police Officer. Like a lot of black recruits who attended the Chicago Police Academy in the early 1980s, I saw a fairly good amount of racism during my training as a CPD recruit. One instructor I recall stated to a number of us in my recruit class, "I grew up in Southern Illinois and we know how to handle you darkies down there." By court decree the City of Chicago was ordered to integrate the rolls of those hired in the class in which I was a member. Black recruits, including me, then became the butt of many jokes during our time in the academy. We would hear some of our instructors shout out frequently among each other, 'hey, has anybody got any whiteout?' None of us said a word knowing that there was no one to report these offensive statements to (Franklin, personal communication, 2019).

THE NEW CENTURY IS NOT DIFFERENT THAN THE LAST

As the new century progressed, apparent controversial policing continued:

- On February 26, 2012, George Zimmerman, a mixed-race neighborhood watch captain in a gated community, killed Trayvon Martin, a teenage black man who was visiting relatives. Zimmerman thought Martin was suspicious and approached him. Prior to and during this deadly action, the police because of rapid events, took a small, but failed protective part. Although there was much controversy before, during and after the shooting, just prior to the shooting a police dispatcher told Zimmerman to stop following Martin, a suspected burglar (CNN Library, 2017). We include this example because remarkably, the acquittal of George Zimmerman, a civilian, not a police officer, for killing Trayvon Martin was the stimulus for the creation of the Black Lives Matter movement.
- Black entrepreneur Eric Garner's life ended on July 17, 2014, on Staten Island, NY, because he was known by police and was suspected of selling untaxed cigarettes. Garner was selling individual cigarettes called 'loosies' at $1 apiece in a depressed neighborhood because New York City's taxation laws were so burdensome that it made buying a pack of cigarettes unaffordable for many residents. The police were dispatched to enforce a taxation violation against this black man in a predominantly black neighborhood. The cost of a pack of cigarettes at the time of Garner's death was around $10. In the summer of 2018, the cost per pack was raised to around $13. While attempting an arrest, he was placed in a chokehold and ultimately stopped breathing. Many were wondering if enforcing a misdemeanor tax violation is the best use of police assets. "Mr. Garner's death was the start

of a succession of police killings that captured national attention and ignited debate over race and law enforcement. From Michael Brown in Ferguson, to Walter Scott in North Charleston, SC., to Freddie Gray in Baltimore, the deaths of black men at the hands of the police have faced a level of scrutiny that would have been unlikely just a year ago. . . ." (Baker et al., 2015)

Less than a month after Garner's death, Michael Brown, a black teenager, was shot and killed on August 9, 2014. Ferguson, MO, Police Officer Darren Wilson spotted Brown along with a friend while walking in the street as he learned an individual matching Brown's description had just stolen tobacco from a food and liquor store. Brown apparently became enraged because of Wilson's presence and began to struggle with Wilson. Witness testimony is conflicting but during the struggle inside and out of the police vehicle, Wilson fired 12 shots hitting Brown at least 9 times, killing him (New York Times, 2015). The killing of Brown and the fact that Officer Wilson was not indicted by a grand jury caused riots in Ferguson. The turmoil lasted for several weeks (Davey & Bosman, 2014) Watching the nightly news it became apparent street thugs and thieves were in their element and caused most of the damage and violence. Adding to the disorder was the presence of armored vehicles.

On October 20, 2014, then Chicago Police Officer Jason Van Dyke shot and killed Laquan MacDonald, a 17-year-old knife-wielding high school student. An initial police report caused officials to conclude the incident was justifiable homicide and no official action against Van Dyke was taken. After an extended period, however, a dash cam video was released that revealed a much different version of the incident than did the official report. "The Illinois State Police Department determined that during the incident Van Dyke fired 16 shots—the full amount his 9 mm semi-automatic pistol held. . . . Van Dyke "was on the scene for less than 30 seconds before he started shooting, in addition to the fact that he starts shooting approximately six seconds after having gotten out of his car," the document notes. "Eight other officers were on the scene, and none of them used their weapons" (Mosendez, 2015). In November 2015, Van Dyke was indicted for first degree murder. In October 2018, Van Dyke was convicted of second-degree murder and in January 2019, he was sentenced to 81 months in prison. In June 2017, three current or former Chicago Police Officers were indicted for obstruction of justice, conspiracy and official misconduct related to their complicity in publication of the alleged, false initial report (Crepeau et al., 2017). Surprisingly, in January 2019, the three officers were acquitted of all charges.

A little over a month after Jason Van Dyke shot and killed Laquan MacDonald, Tamir Rice was shot and killed on November 22, 2014, by a Cleveland, OH, officer. Rice, a 12-year-old black male, was playing with a pellet gun. Although the caller told the police dispatcher that the weapon was probably fake, the two officers who responded were not told of the fact. The officers were criticized for pulling up too close to the subject, putting themselves in plausible danger, and shooting the boy within seconds of arrival. Later it was discovered the officer who shot Rice resigned from a neighboring department before being fired because of insubordination, lying and being emotionally unstable. A declination of indictment caused a national outrage because this and like incidents involving young black men (Fortin & Bromwich 2017).

On April 2, 2015, Eric Harris, a 44-year-old black man, was shot and killed during a gun-sale sting. Harris was shot by Tulsa County, OK, reserve deputy Robert Charles Bates, a retired insurance executive and friend of the (then) County Sheriff, Stanley Glanz. He was fatally shot when Bates apparently mistook his handgun for a nonlethal Taser (Johnson, 2016). "First and foremost," (Bates) said, "let me apologise (sic) to the family of Eric Harris. . . . Harris's brother, Andre, said on Monday he did not believe the shooting had "anything to do with race," like others around the U.S. recently involving white police officers and unarmed black men, which have led to sustained controversy, protest and debate over police attitudes towards racial minorities" (The Guardian, 2015). This incident, however, does show the indifference shown in some departments for ample training for all officers.

On April 4, 2015, two days later, Walter Scott, a 50-year-old black man, was shot by a North Charleston, SC, police officer for resisting arrest. Scott was shot in the back while running away. Officer Michael Slager was charged with murder in state court, but the charges were dropped when he pled guilty to a federal charge of deprivation of rights under the color of law i.e., a civil rights violation (Yan et al.,

2017). Slager was subsequently sentenced to 20 years in federal prison.

Another death of a black man caused considerable civil disorder in Baltimore, MD. The *Rolling Stone* [magazine] reported that "On April 12, 2015, a 25-year-old black man from the west side of Baltimore named Freddie Gray was arrested for possession of a "switchblade," put inside a Baltimore Police Department (BPD) transport van, and then, 45 minutes later, was found unconscious and not breathing, his spinal cord nearly severed. Following a seven-day coma, Gray died on April 19th; his untimely death and citizen video of his arrest, which showed Gray screaming in pain, prompted both the peaceful protests and headline-grabbing riots. The subsequent two-week police investigation ultimately concluded that Gray's injury happened sometime during the van's route — over six stops, with two prisoner checks, and another passenger pick-up" (McDonell-Parry & Barron, 2017). The Baltimore City State's Attorney's office subsequently filed criminal charges against six city officers. In the following two years four officers would be found not guilty and the charges were dropped for two others (McDonell-Parry & Barron, 2017).

On July 6, 2016, Philando Castile was shot and killed by St. Anthony, MN, police officer Jeronimo Yanez, when Castile's vehicle was stopped for broken taillights. Castile announced to Officer Yanez, "Sir, I have to tell you, I do have a firearm on me." (Al Jazeera Media Network, 2017). After telling Castile not to pull it out, Officer Yanez shot him. Castile's girlfriend said the officer had just asked for his license and registration. It was later learned, Castile, a school cafeteria worker, was legally permitted to carry the weapon.

On February 23, 2020, Ahmaud Arbery was killed by two white men and an accomplice when Arbery was suspected of burglary. We include his death because of the ensuing media attention and one of the suspects is a former law enforcement officer.

On May 25, 2020, George Floyd was arrested in Minneapolis, MN, because he was suspected of making a purchase with a counterfeit $20 bill. As Floyd was taken into custody he was placed on the ground and, as clearly seen on a video, an officer's knee was used to further restrain him. As Floyd pleaded with the officer that he could not breathe, he died. Two autopsies found that Floyd died by homicide.

Not all shootings by police are controversial. In 2017, 987 people were shot and killed by police. Of that total 457 were white, 223 were black, 179 were Hispanic and 128 were categorized as 'other' or 'unknown' (*The Washington Post,* n.d.). No matter what the statistics, there is still acrimony between the police and the black community.

TWO-TIERED JUSTICE: ONE FOR BLACKS AND THE BEST FOR WHITES

There has been much discussion about a two-tiered justice system in the United States. Tough on crime advocates have passed laws sentencing violators of minor narcotics offenses to a minimum of 5 years in a heavily guarded prison. Conversely, politicians, the politically connected and the more affluent seemingly are sentenced for a shorter period for stealing millions, affecting thousands while being housed in a prison commonly called a 'country club'. Less has been discussed about how police officers respond to people of different cultures and races.

Many years ago, I was assigned to the 018th District which was and for the most part still is full of bars and nightclubs. From my experience in the district I know there is a two-tiered system of law enforcement, at least there was in the Chicago Police Department (Franklin, personal communication).

When I was a patrolman in the 018th District, a new club opened up near our old station on Chicago Ave. near LaSalle Street on the Northside of Chicago. I will call it the Nightspot. It was a decidedly black crowd. It was known that the few majority black clientele clubs always garnered extra scrutiny from the 018th District police. Large crowds of black males or just black males walking around in the mostly white Gold Coast or River North area made many of the regular bar hoppers and residents nervous. Part of our unspoken duties was to relieve the residents of their fears/concerns (Franklin, personal communication).

The watch commander, a lieutenant, made it clear during roll calls that he felt personally uncomfortable with this club operating within such a close vicinity to our police station. He made it clear that he expected all of us to pay special attention to the club, closely monitor its clientele and to "write everything and everyone you can find" within the vicinity of the club. We all knew what that meant and it was made crystal clear to all of us who were assigned to that watch; give everyone coming to or leaving from the club a 'heavy police presence,' with no breaks whatsoever for any infractions observed (Franklin, personal communication).

The Nightspot along with clubs with a white clientele would give occasional grief to the officers who patrolled the area. Fights would break out, both inside or out; clientele were robbed as they left and attempted to make their way back to their vehicles unmolested. One night the security crew of a long-established white club on Division Street had a private party. That evening they came out of the club drunk and beat up more than a few on-duty officers. There was no move by the city to suspend their liquor license and no financial penalties were assessed, even though many of the white security crew were arrested and faced serious charges (Franklin, personal communication).

The Nightspot, the black club, continued to be given special attention. Eventually, the city licensing bureau brought so much pressure to bear upon the club, the owners voluntarily turned in their liquor license to the city of Chicago and the club was shuttered (Franklin, personal communication).

Another example of the two-tiered system I experienced is when I was assigned as a sergeant to the Organized Crime Division/ Narcotics Section. My team conducted the usual buy/busts, narcotic complaint investigations, the execution of search warrants and a few extensive narcotics conspiracy investigations. As I was leaving for the day, another team needed help and I was asked to arrange for a prisoner transport. As I arrived to supervise the transport, I soon determined that the adult, black female prisoner was held in detention for over 6 hours without being given either food or drink. She was also dressed inappropriately to leave her apartment, for transport or public view. She was embarrassed to be in such a state, and it was as embarrassing for others to see her. Although she was arrested for possession of narcotics with intent to distribute, the prisoner's care and wellbeing was the duty of the arresting officers. When I approached the responsible sergeant, he told me she did not cause any problems for the officers and he did not know why she was not fed or in such unsuitable dress because he was 'just the supervisor'. It is difficult for me to describe my anger (Franklin, personal communication).

Over time I have seen hundreds of prisoners of all races brought into department facilities. Not once have I seen a white female prisoner in such disarray. It is well documented the department has always had a two-tiered system of discipline; what has had less discussion is the department's sometimes two-tiered system of law enforcement (Franklin, personal communication).

REFLECTIONS OF A BLACK MOTHER AND A WHITE COP

Black parents bare a burden many other parents do not. Black parents must give their children the 'talk.' Not a talk like white parents give about honesty, responsibility and the birds and bees, but the additional duty of ensuring their children know how to act, what to say and certainly what not to do when confronted by a police officer.

In his book, *Breaking rank: a top cop's exposé of the dark side of American policing* (2005), Norm Stamper presents the following:

> Momma and Daddy were lucky, they had girls. I had boys. My boys are eleven and nine now, and I'm scared to death for them. It's not that I'm afraid they're gonna get jumped into a gang, or wind up doing or dealing drugs. No sir. My big fear is they're gonna run into one of you people one night and they won't be coming home. It's like open season on young black men in our community, like they're walking around with targets on their backs. I have a recurring nightmare, Chief: I get this call in the middle of the night, "Come on down to the morgue, Mrs. Johnson, We got one of your boys here. Police shot him when he tried to run." (Stamper, 2005)

An African American mother at a community forum. Then there is the radically contrasting view of a police officer:

> It's open season on us in the Heights, Chief. If you're working the blacks you're wearing a target, plain and simple. For me it comes down to this: kill or be killed. I got a wife and two boys. My sons need their father. I'm gonna do whatever it takes to make it home at the end of the shift. (Stamper, 2005)

It is apparent the African American mother and the white cop are looking for protection. The white cop knows from training and experience he has plenty of protections, but he also knows sometimes plenty is not enough. At the same time the black community like any community, like the average American knows little about the law and how it protects them. Doug Wylle from PoliceOne.com in an updated article published in February 2020, titled: *5 Supreme Court cases the police and the public should know* explained some of the protections afforded citizens and police by the U.S. Supreme Court.

The first case, Graham v. Connor, 490 U.S. 386 (1989), established an 'objectively reasonable standard' when use of force is judged rather than the use of hindsight. This decision actually gives more protection to a police officer but an associated decision, Tennessee v. Garner, 471 U.S.1 (1985), gives greater protection to any citizen. In *Garner,* an officer may not use deadly force on a fleeing suspect unless there is probable cause that the suspect poses a significant threat to the officer or others. Periodically an officer is charged with homicide because of this decision. Prior to *Garner* many jurisdictions allowed an officer to shoot any fleeing suspect regardless of the threat posed.

Terry v. Ohio, 392 U.S.1 (1968), is a Supreme Court decision that protects both citizen and officer. Stop and frisk is a lawful practice although misunderstood by many citizens. An officer can perform a pat down or surface search if the officer has reasonable suspicion that the person has committed, is committing or is about to commit a crime and may be armed and dangerous. The stop-and-frisk program in New York City continues to cause controversy because of recognized racial profiling and political posturing.

Another, even earlier decision, Weeks v. United States, 232 U.S. 383 (1914), established that evidence seized by federal agents in violation of the Fourth Amendment could not be used in a criminal prosecution. *Weeks* created the 'exclusionary rule' while another decision, Silverthorne Lumber Co. Inc. v. United States, 251 U. S. 385 (1920), added the 'fruits of the poisonous tree' which means any evidence gained under the exclusionary rule is tainted and also cannot be used in a prosecution. A more well-known decision. Mapp v. Ohio, 367 U.S. 643 (1961), extended both protections to all jurisdictions, not just federal.

Finally, Carroll v. United States, 267 U.S 132 (1925), established an automobile exception to Fourth Amendment protections to warrantless searches. Considering a vehicle is mobile, if an officer has probable cause that it contains evidence of a crime, the vehicle can be searched without a warrant. Many citizens may ask how a warrantless search can protect them, but proactive police searches protect the community and maintains order.

In spite of the above protections and many more, many believe the shootings of an inordinate number of unarmed black males or a lengthy history of abuse of suspects is not just a coincidence in the fast-paced life and split second decisions some make in enforcing the law. Director of the ACLU Racial Justice Program Dennis Baker, scrutinizing only two shootings, Eric Harris and Walter Scott, suggests the shootings "both depict the killing of unarmed Black men as a result of what appears to be an unjustified and unnecessary use of force. . . . But looking at each incident in its entirety suggests that the problems run far deeper than mere accidents or miscalculations that occur in a split second under extreme stress. Instead, both cases demonstrate a distinct callousness and insensitivity, which suggest that the stage for these killings may have been set long before shots were actually fired." Actions and statements suggest that there is a fundamental disregard for humanity by some officers (Parker, 2015). In American policing there is an apparent lack of deep-rooted training and a wealth of readily seen and implicit bias.

REFERENCES

Al Jazeera Media Network. (2017). Philando Castile killings: Police video sparks outrage. http://www.aljazeera.com/news/2017/06/philando-castile-killing-police-video-sparks-outrage-170621051241173.html

Baker, A., Goodman, D.J., & Mueller, B. (2015). Beyond the chokehold: the path to Eric Garner's death. *The New York Times*. https://www.nytimes.com/2015/06/14/nyregion/eric-garner-police-chokehold-staten-island.html

Brownson, J. (2017). Can't we all just get along? *Huff Post. The Blog*.

CNN Library. (2017). Trayvon Martin shooting fast facts. http://www.cnn.com/2013/06/05/us/trayvon-martin-shooting-fast-facts/index.html

Crain, C. (2020). What a white-supremacist coup looks like. *The New Yorker, Books Issue*, pp. 2, 5, 9. https://www.newyorker.com/magazine/2020/04/27/what-a-white-supremacist-coup-looks-like

Crepeau, M., Hinkel, D., Meisner, J., & Gorner, J. (2017). Three Chicago cops indicted in alleged cover-up of Laquan McDonald shooting details. *Chicago Tribune*. http://www.cnn.com/2017/06/27/us/chicago-officers-indicted-laquan-mcdonald/index.html

Davey, M., & Bosman, J. (2014). Protests flair after Ferguson police officer is not indicted. *The New York Times*. https://www.nytimes.com/2014/11/25/us/ferguson-darren-wilson-shooting-michael-brown-grand-jury.html#

Fortin, J., & Bromwich, J. E. (2017). Cleveland police officer who shot Tamir Rice is fired. *The New York Times*. https://www.nytimes.com/2017/05/30/us/cleveland-police-tamir-rice.html

Grunlund, M. (2017). Abner Luoima: 20 years since infamous attach by ex-cop Justin Volpe. *Staten Island Real-Time News. Silive.com.* http://www.npr.org/2017/04/26/524744989/when-la-erupted-in-anger-a-look-back-at-the-rodney-king-riots

Guardian, The. (2015). Tulsa officer who fatally shot Eric Harris 'regrets' using gun instead of Taser. https://www.theguardian.com/us-news/2015/apr/17/tulsa-oklahoma-police-shooting-robert-bates-eric-harris-apology

Johnson, A. (2016). Tulsa reserve deputy convicted of manslaughter in death of Eric Harris. NBC News. https://www.nbcnews.com/news/us-news/tulsa-reserve-deputy-convicted-manslaughter-death-eric-harris-n563836

Kappeler, V. E., Ph.D. (2014). A brief history of slavery and the origins of American policing. Eastern Kentucky University police studies online, p. 1. http://plsonline.eku.edu/insidelook/brief-history-slavery-and-origins-american-policing

McDonell-Parry, A., & Barron, J. (2017). Death of Freddie Gray: 5 things you didn't know. *Rolling Stone.* http://www.rollingstone.com/culture/features/death-of-freddie-gray-5-things-you-didnt-know-w476107

Moodie-Mills, D. (2017). The 'Green Book' was a travel guide just for black motorists. NBC News. https://www.nbcnews.com/news/nbcblk/green-book-was-travel-guide-just-black-motorists-n649081

Mosendz, P. (2015). Chicago officials release video of white police officer shooting black teenager. *Newsweek.* http://www.newsweek.com/chicago-police-officer-charged-murder-black-teenager-398031

National Public Radio. (2017). When L.A. erupted in anger: a look back at the Rodney King riots. http://www.npr.org/2017/04/26/524744989/when-la-erupted-in-anger-a-look-back-at-the-rodney-king-riots

New York Times, The. (2015). What happened in Ferguson? https://www.nytimes.com/interactive/2014/08/13/us/ferguson-missouri-town-under-siege-after-police-shooting.html

Nunnelly, W. A., (1991). *Bull Connor.* Tuscaloosa, AL: University of Alabama Press, p. 162.

Parker, D. (2015). Recent slayings of unarmed black men showcase culture of police violence. American Civil Liberties Union. https://www.aclu.org/blog/racial-justice/race-and-criminal-justice/recent-slayings-unarmed-black-men-showcase-culture

Pilgram, D., Ph.D. (2012). The garbage man: why I collect racist objects. Farris State University, Jim Crow Museum of Racist Memorabilia. https://www.ferris.edu/HTMLS/news/jimcrow/collect.htm

Stamper, N. (2005). *Breaking rank: a top cop's expose' of the dark side of American policing.* New York: Nation Books.

Tayler, G. Flint. (2012). A long and winding road: the struggle for justice in the Chicago police torture cases. People's Law Office. *Loyola Public Interest Reporter.* Loyola University, Chicago. http://peopleslawoffice.com/wp-content/uploads/2012/06/A-long-and-winding-road-for-justice-in-chicago-police-torture-civil-rights-cases.pdf

Tunnell, H. (2014). The Negro motorist green book (1936-1964). BlackPast.org. Online Reference Guide to African American History. https://blackpast.org/aah/negro-motorist-green-book-1936-1964

Washington Post, The. (n.d.). Fatal force. https://www.washingtonpost.com/graphics
  /national/police-shootings-2017/

Yan, H., Khushbu, S., & Grinberg, E. (2017). Ex-officer Michael Slager pleads guilty
  to shooting death of Walter Scott. *Cable News Network*. http://www.cnn.com
  /2017/05/02/us/michael-slager-federal-plea/index.html

Chapter Two

HOW WIDE IS THE DIVIDE?

We cannot solve our problems with the same thinking we used when we created them.

Albert Einstein

Adding to the ongoing bitterness between the police and the black community, another controversy emerged over the apparent sympathy shown to the Austin, Texas bomber who killed himself rather than be arrested by the encircling police. The bomber, Mark Anthony Conditt, was a troubled 23-year-old white man who terrorized the Austin area during March 2018, detonating several homemade bombs that killed two people and injured several others. Additional acrimony to people of color was apparent when Austin Police Chief Brian Manley described a cellphone recording left by the bomber "as an outcry of a very challenged young man." Many observers took this statement as a show of compassion for a killer when less, if any, is shown for innocent black men shot and killed by police. "Here you have a case of a young white male who killed and injured people of color, and we're culturally more concerned about his story, about his life, about what led him to take these lives," said David Leonard, professor in the department of critical culture, gender and race studies at Washington State University. "It's a striking reminder of a racial empathy gap that persists" (Hajela, 2018). The divide, the strong dislike, even hatred between people of color and law enforcement officers continues.

WHAT DID YOUR DADDY DO?

As we have learned, the root cause of this bitterness with American policing goes back hundreds of years. Over the years blacks were considered second class or less by whites, some were slaves, most were from countries with less resources than others. It is difficult to discuss the differences between races, but there is a divide. Different cultures and different people in those cultures have different values, different ways of thinking, of analyzing, of reacting to different stimuli.

In 2018, CNN reported that police around the country have been called to investigate all sorts of non-criminal, commonplace activities, but with one peculiar characteristic. The distinction is police have been called to question members of the black community for among many other normal routine things as:

- Golfing too slowly
- Barbequing at a park
- Working out at a gym
- Not waving when leaving an Airbnb
- Redeeming a coupon
- Eating lunch on a college campus
- Riding in a car with a white grandmother
- Babysitting two white children
- Working as a firefighter
- Shopping while pregnant
- Driving with tree leaves on a car

As absurd as these examples are, we only gave you the short list of what CNN reported (Griggs, 2018).

Practitioners of socioeconomics say economic and social factors may play a role in the way one reasons. Socioeconomic status is the social standing or class of an individual or group. It is often measured as a combination of education, income and occupation. The American Psychological Association says inspections of the socioeconomic status of individuals may uncover inequities in the ability to obtain resources, not including issues related to privilege, power and control. This status can affect a wide range of outcomes in one's life. Socioeconomic status (SES) does not just include income or the lack of it, but financial stability, opportunities in and quality of life, educational successes or failures and one's own impression or attitude regarding their lot in life. Socioeconomic status can affect a person's mental and physical health and their academic skills and progression (Saegert et al., 2006). It may even affect how one worships the Lord.

ALL IN THE NAME OF THE LORD

John M. Perkins is cofounder of the Christian Community Development Association. He is also the founder and president emeritus of the John and Vera Mae Perkins Foundation for Reconciliation, Justice, and Christian Community Development. He has been involved in the civil rights movement most of his life. Perkins believes black and white Christian faith may seem the same; it is closely related, but in reality there is a divide when thinking about justice and redemption. According to Perkins white theology favors a personal viewpoint of redemption. "Emphasis has been placed on evangelism [publicly preaching or missionaries], salvation, and individual spiritual growth and holiness—with the Bible being regarded as a devotional book that inspires believers individually" (Perkins 2017). Black theology, on the other hand, has a contrasting view on redemption partially because much of black theology was developed because of white opposition. African American theology is based on liberation, on the model of Moses—"Let my people Go!" Perkins says whites believe black theology is strange (Perkins, 2017).

What also is different about black theology is that it places a differing emphasis on justice. Perkins goes on to say that the "Old Testament justice laws aren't just about punishing sin, they're also about preventing oppression" (Perkins, 2017). Each person in the community should be cared for and given a chance for success. According to Perkins it is God's desire that poor people should have the means to feed themselves and opportunities to break away from debt. Although some churches have embraced this kind of social justice, he believes society has yet to fully grasp this concept. It seems Perkins does not believe social programs with all their help and funding is enough to help the poor or the homeless. He advocates more churches, all churches, take the step to embrace the exploited and disenfranchised and give them the needed support to raise themselves above their current social and economic station.

Not only do some in the black community think differently about justice and redemption, but they also might think differently when celebrating life. Kwanzaa is an African American celebration observed in the United States just after Christmas day through January 1st. It was created in 1966 by Dr. Maulana Karenga, the chairman of African Studies at California State University. The holiday was created in response to the Los Angeles Watts Riots which occurred in 1965 and continues to bring African Americans together as a community. Kwanzaa has seven core principles:

- To maintain unity in the family, community, nation and race.
- To define ourselves, accomplish and speak without help from others.
- To accomplish things and solve problems as a community.
- To build and control our own economic future.
- Collectively to restore the community to its traditional greatness.
- To leave the community a better place than it was when we entered it.
- To believe in ourselves, parents, teachers, leaders and the righteousness and victory of our struggle. (Official Kwanzaa Website, 2020)

Perkins also believes the tension between whites and blacks is apparent. The pressure could be seen in Ferguson after Michael Brown was shot by a white police officer. He goes on to say the white community saw the riots in Ferguson as too strong a reaction by blacks for a perceived wrong. Conversely, the black community reacted as it did because blacks have been oppressed too long and legislation has not, in reality, improved the lives of the exploited. He also believes neither side is listening to the other. Both sides are shouting and no one is listening (Perkins 2017).

Along with the white community, John Perkins also places blame on black Christian practice for division between the races. He believes blacks expect the white community to show contrition by their works. Through Jesus's teachings we all must understand why forgiveness is fundamental to the way we relate to others. The only way to release hostility and division among the races, all races, is to repent and forgive (Perkins, 2017).

REDISTRIBUTION–WHAAT?

Perkins believes in being a good neighbor. Being a good neighbor goes beyond caring for them, it also means strengthening them. Perkins, along with a small group, developed something they call the three R's, not the three R's that everyone knows from elementary school: reading, [w]riting and 'rithmetic, but relocation, reconciliation, and redistribution. The three R's will bring people together as good neighbors. The meaning of relocation is not just moving locations, but according to Perkins, "becoming involved in the community, knowing your neighbors, and being aware of the issues that confront them . . ." (Perkins, 2017). Relocation means being a voice for the voiceless. The second word of the three R's is reconciliation that means change, agreement, coming together and forgiveness.

The third word in the trilogy is redistribution which is a dirty word to many: taking from the more affluent and giving to the less fortunate. However, in this instance it does not mean taking from the rich and giving to the poor. In fact, Perkins does not believe the idea would work.

According to The Center for Budget and Policy Priorities about 9% of the federal budget in 2017, or $357 billion, supported programs to help individuals and families who face hardship. However, this figure is disputed because of the many programs included and who those programs benefit (Center on Budget and Policy Priorities, 2019).

What Perkins' definition of redistribution does include is opportunities. As Perkins says, "Too much free stuff undermines people's dignity and feelings of value. The value is more appreciated when it comes out of one's own effort. . . . Unfortunately, America's current welfare system creates dependency and entitlement. Homeless shelters and food pantries are doing a good job helping people . . . [but] they don't offer training for jobs or ways to connect people to work" (Perkins, 2017). Perkins proposes that the business sector "provide job opportunities and fund nonprofits that can offer training schools for those who have never worked before. This is real redistribution: the people with the most skills and opportunities sharing with those who don't have them" (Perkins, 2017).

Interestingly, it seems the young adults, the survivors of the Marjory Stoneman Douglas High School shooting that took place in Parkland, Florida on February 12, 2018, the creators of the

#NeverAgain movement, are using, surely unknowingly, Perkins' three R's to be good neighbors. The movement has called for a renewed assault-weapons ban, comprehensive background checks for gun buyers and computerized gun-ownership records. The first R, relocation, is bringing people together, mostly high school students, many of whom are not able to vote, but who want to be good neighbors, to be a voice for the voiceless. Concerning reconciliation, #NeverAgain fosters coming together for change and is in agreement with many who are against gun violence and for gun reform (Alter, 2018).

In a recent study by PolitiFact, it was discovered that in Wisconsin, depending on what survey was highlighted, 84% to 94% of adults or registered voters favored background checks for all gun buyers. The surveys were conducted by Quinnipiac University (94%), Washington University and American Panel Survey (84%), CBS News (89%), Morning Consult (86%), Public Policy Polling (84%), and CBS News/New York Times (88%) (Kertscher, 2017).

The third and final R does not stand for unearned opportunities or the sharing of wealth but for redistributing power, strength and authority. The #NeverAgain movement has received millions of dollars from grassroots donors and from high-profile celebrities. The group is also receiving assistance from a high-profile public relations firm and several seasoned groups to further their cause. The young adults are also coordinating with other like-minded groups because they know many organizations are striving for the same results: the safety of all (Perkins, 2017).

IS JUSTICE EQUALITY?

What John M. Perkins is advocating is justice for all. A clergyman who will remain anonymous believes justice is the quality of doing right, doing what is good or proper. Justice is the ability to reason with truth and facts to develop an outcome free from error. Justice is an economic and stewardship issue. "How we utilize the resources we've been given determines whether we have been just" (Anonymous, personal communication, 2018). "For the Lord is a God of Justice" (Isaiah, 30:18, the New King James Version). The anonymous clergyman believes black Christians practice their religion to uplift people and the Bible is considered a textbook for living. He goes on to say:

"Black theology does not specify that the races should be separate but, sadly, it has turned out that way. White theology poisoned the stream when the word, 'racial,' was added to the reconciliation aspect of the gospel in an effort to accommodate racism. Some churches found it inappropriate or even evil to engage their congregation to protest injustice. Many Christians do just enough social good in the black community to salve their conscience while maintaining imperialistic theology. They do just enough to get by without repentance. There is an anger expressed by blacks that helps to change the world, and it is an anger that is openly expressed. The world would have been denied new freedoms if it were not for the anger of William Wilberforce, a 16th century anti-slave leader, Nelson Mandela, Martin Luther King, Jr., and many others. But today, the shooting of black men by police and the riots the shootings have caused, demonstrates the anger and the fact that the police and the people calling for change are not listening to each other" (Anonymous, personal communication, 2018).

The clergyman who wanted to stay anonymous goes on to say, "In the 1960s, I was a young deacon in training and sent to be a pastor in an all-black Episcopal Church in a southern state. It was a year-long assignment and at its conclusion I was ordained in the Episcopal Church. This was a time during integration in the Deep South. As a white clergy, a stranger, I was taken into the church family to be their leader. I came as a 'gleaner,' one who learns little by little, but I was accepted to share their lives. My wife played the 'pipe organ,' and taught Sunday school. We experienced redemption and justice during a time of racism all around us. We were blessed." (Anonymous, personal communication, 2018) Being fair can be just and a fulfillment of compassionate treatment. "Be Merciful, just as your Father is merciful" (St. Luke) 6:36. Justice is not equality, but justice can bring fairness.

THERE IS EQUALITY AND THEN THERE IS JUSTICE

The United States was created with the fundamental principle that 'all men are created equal'. Equality is a status that offers the same rights and opportunities. Race equality can mean giving the same treatment to others; showing respect to all equally. Being equal is a reality that can be affected by one's state of mind or attitude. One might be treated as an equal, but the person might believe otherwise because of a learned prevailing tendency. A white person might believe a black person is being treated equally while the black person believes the opposite. Addressing reality, no one is really treated equally because of friendships, family ties, politics, work ethic, and of course, bias. A worker who goes beyond the norm to complete a task, certainly is not treated, nor should be treated the same as an average co-worker. So, equality should offer rights, opportunities and treatment but under certain circumstances; everyone is not the same. Those circumstances have to do with justice.

Being just is being fair. For justice to be served truth must be understood and acted upon. Justice or being fair is taking into account all aspects, elements and circumstances and taking appropriate action. We have all heard the expression, 'that's not fair.' Fairness can be subjective and be interpreted differently by different people. But to obtain fairness, it must be objective, evenhanded, and open-minded. It is honest and unbiased. It would be unfair to treat co-workers equally when their work ethic and production is different. To treat everyone equally would be an injustice. However, justice demands that everyone be given the same rights and opportunities. Fairness enters the picture when each individual decides what to do with their rights and opportunities.

THE STRUGGLE OVER FAIRNESS

As much disagreement as there is among the races, there is one truth that is understood by all: too many black men and women are dying by the hands of police. Some are criminals who decide their own fate while others are innocent and should have lived another day. What the Black Lives Matter movement has attempted to do is interrupt the dilemma between races and force another step to pseudo equality. We say pseudo because any attempts at equality between the races have always been an attempt and will continue to be attempts at equality.

Even before the British Slavery Abolition Act of 1833 that was made more than a section in a history book by the movie Amazing Grace in 2006, Denmark prohibited slaves in the West Indies in 1803 (Reuters, 2007). Both countries reached a milestone for the world. In the United States many anti-slavery efforts were made as early as the late 1700s. A milestone was reached, however, when the Thirteenth Amendment to the U.S. Constitution ratified by the states in December 1865, abolished slavery. Another major milestone was the civil rights movement of the 1950s and 60s that caused considerable federal legislation in the 1960s. The Civil Rights Act of 1964 prohibited discrimination in public accommodations and employment based on race, color, religion or national origin. The Voting Rights Act of 1965 protected the right to vote. The Immigration and Nationality Services Act of 1965 allowed immigration from groups [persons of color] other than those from traditional [white] European countries. The Fair Housing Act of 1968 prohibited discrimination in sales and rentals (Florida National University, 2016). The Black Lives Matter movement is the most current civil rights milestone in American history. As we know the movement has caused many in American politics and policing to re-evaluate policies and actions and the trust they generate from citizens served.

HOW FAIR IS THE JUSTICE SYSTEM?

Some citizens in our society rebel against a system they do not trust. It can be said the justice system is one item on a long list of disappointments experienced by many people of color. Any community wants laws and a system to enforce them that offers fairness and is just; is decent and honest to anyone who enters it. Therefore, it is necessary for punishment to impose suffering for a violation of law, but justice, on the other hand, must judge an offender's moral blameworthiness; an offender's responsibility in the law violation along with the seriousness of the offense. Paul H. and Sarah M. Robinson believe if a system is considered fair by the community, the community will be more inclined to accept punishment. But punishment must be considered deserved, not overly harsh. Retaliation for a crime must be 'an eye for an eye' or 'a tooth for a tooth.' Punishment must match the crime. Without deserved punishment, community cooperation with law enforcement can be difficult, but to promote a fair and just system can bring a demonstration of greater cooperation (Robinson & Robinson, 2015).

For punishment to match the crime, legitimate mitigations must be considered to avoid punishment that is undeserved. A community may consider increased cooperation with the system if an offender with greater culpability is given more punishment than one who is less responsible. A system that promotes justice and avoids injustice earns credibility, but the leadership of politicians, the police chief and anyone in the criminal justice system must also be credible. Accepted leadership must promote goals that are consistent with citizen desires, with their sense of justice; there must be shared judgments. Shunning citizen desires and the lack of credible, accepted leadership can promote active resistance to and disrespect for the system (Robinson & Robinson, 2015).

Surprisingly, many common law rules and U.S. Supreme Court decisions have caused some citizens to question the fairness and justice found in the criminal justice system (Robinson & Robinson, 2015).

The felony murder rule and vicarious liability holds that an accomplice to a crime can be held accountable for murder even if the accomplice was not the killer. This doctrine is controversial because an accomplice can be held accountable for aiding the murderer even without being present or having knowledge of what was about to occur. Potentially, the rule places a member of the community in danger of prosecution even having no knowledge of the crime.

The Three Strikes Law found in more than 50% of states mandates an offender serve, arguably, an unreasonable amount of time in prison for a third felony offense. Some sentences for a third offense, even for a minor theft with no bodily harm, might be life in prison. Some believe the Three Strikes Law disproportionally punishes third-time offenders because they are being given preventive detention to stop them for crimes they might commit in the future denying them due process. Many in the community believe the law is unfair and unjust. In late 2018, U.S. Congress passed the First Step Act which eases the federal three strikes rule.

Mapp v. Ohio, 376 U.S. 643 is a 1961 U.S. Supreme Court decision that excludes evidence in state and federal courts that was seized in violation of the Fourth Amendment that protects unreasonable searches and seizures. Arguably, the 'exclusionary rule' decision protects citizens from police excesses, but also places the public in harm's way by affording an offender a greater effort by the criminal justice system to prove guilt.

Closely related to the exclusionary rule is the 'fruit of the poisonous tree' principle. The phrase is a figure of speech used to describe evidence that is generally not admissible in court because the evidence was acquired from a previous unreasonable search, illegal arrest or intimidation that led officers to this additional evidence. As is the exclusionary rule, the poisonous tree doctrine is based on deterring police officers from violating a person's constitutional rights. Again, this doctrine places the public in harm's way by requiring the prosecution to take greater steps to prove guilt.

Miranda v. Arizona, 384 U.S. 436, is a 1966 U.S. Supreme Court ruling that created the Miranda warning. The decision required that incriminating statements can be used only at trial if the defendant was aware of his right to counsel [Sixth Amendment to the U.S. Constitution] and his right against self-incrimination [Fifth Amendment]. (Hein, 2013) In exigent circumstances a police officer may decide not to read a suspect's rights warning, but in doing so forfeits the opportunity to use any incriminating statements in a prosecution. However, the officer may use the information provided by the suspect to protect the community. Some believe the Miranda warning allows too many lawbreakers to escape just punishment and is one of many failures of the justice system.

THE SYSTEM MUST PROTECT THE
ACCUSED BUT ALSO THE VICTIM

For a community to consider the justice system to be legitimate the role of a court should be one to determine whether the proceedings as a whole are fair. The rights of the victim and of the community must be as important as the rights of the accused. Arguably, the plea bargain is used by a prosecutor to operate within a set budget, certainly not to promote a fair and just system. Criminal justice should not be played as a chess game where the smartest, most experienced attorney with the most resources has leverage over the opposition with less intellectual or monetary ability. One can understand the importance of the Bill of Rights, but certainly one can also see ways of achieving justice while maintaining the credibility of the criminal justice system (Robinson & Robinson, 2015). Differences between the races continue.

WHAT TO DO ABOUT THE DIVIDE?

I spoke to a black woman, a supporter of the Black Lives Matter movement, who told me about experiences only a black person would know. She said a white person will never know what it is like to live in a black neighborhood, or to travel to a white area being black. Police, all police, whether white or black treat the black community differently than other races. There is a wide disparity between how white and black areas are policed. There is a huge disparity between how police approach and treat blacks. It is her experience that blacks are always suspect and police generally treat blacks with contempt and disrespect.

She said we all know there are a large number of areas in the United States that are segregated. Segregated areas were created by bigotry with the help of redlining, a now illegal practice. Illegal, but still used in more subtle ways. In years past, redlining was the methodical denial of honest real estate services, mortgage loans and insurance if a person of color dared to attempt to move to an area not open to blacks. Because of redlining many areas are identified as white, black or Asian neighborhoods. Because of that concentration and the fact whites have a poor perception of blacks, in general, police are more aggressive with a black person, any black person.

Although there may be a higher incidence of crime in some black areas, she said blacks are not anti-social as many people might believe. A black person might seem to be anti-social only because of their response to disrespect. Black crime seems to be high-lighted in the news media while black accomplishment not so much.

Recalling the Sandra Bland arrest and suicide in 2015, I viewed two videos, one released soon after her arrest and suicide and one released in 2019. Both show the encounter and arrest of Sandra Bland by a Texas State Trooper from two perspectives—one from the trooper's dash cam and one from Bland's iphone apparently sitting on the front seat of her car. The dash cam shows the trooper stopping Bland's car and at first professionally interacting with her, but Bland almost immediately began using a sarcastic tone of voice. Bland quickly became rude and argumentative. The interaction quickly became a strong confrontation. The video, taken by Bland's iphone, shows her becoming excited, arguing and reluctantly exiting her vehicle, while angrily asking the trooper why she was pulled over. In her excited state she was verbally combative, uncooperative and belligerent. In response the trooper become angry and domineering and arrested Bland (Hein, personal communication, 2019).

The black woman I spoke to perceived the interaction in a somewhat different perspective than I did. She told me that describing Bland's behavior as belligerent is stereotypical and racist. She stated there was nothing wrong with Bland asking why she was pulled over or what she did which caused the trooper to ask her to leave her vehicle. She said Bland had a confrontation with the officer because people with a darker skin tone are never allowed to question authority. A drunk white man going toe to toe verbally with an officer never gets tasered or shot. She explained to me that black people are always listed as a threat, belligerent, large and scary. The woman told me the trooper became frustrated and was wrong to take the action he did, that Bland was not afraid of the trooper, but the trooper was afraid of Bland. Sandra Bland was arrested and several days later while in jail, she committed suicide.

The interviewee said Bland learned to be distrustful of police while living in Chicago and as a new transplant was apprehensive of southern police. She told me in her day, the 'talk' about how to interact with a police officer was only given to boys, but now the 'talk' is given to both boys and girls. But, as the black community becomes more aware of their rights, many blacks will no longer sit idle and allow an officer to bully them.

The woman I interviewed thought Bland spoke up for herself and she honestly believes Bland did nothing wrong. I agree Bland spoke up for herself and pleaded with the troop to give her a ticket. I believe Bland did everything wrong, but if I was the trooper I would have diffused the situation as best I could. The trooper became aggressive almost immediately. I do not believe the trooper was properly trained.

Bland committed suicide in her jail cell several days after she was arrested. The interviewee told me she also suspects Bland did not commit suicide; she never believed the suicide story. She said Bland was in a cell near a back door and in the cell with her was a black garbage bag. She questions the presence of the bag because she believes it is odd for a black plastic bag to be in a jail cell (Hein, personal communication, 2019).

John C. Franklin offers a different perspective. I won't say that black women are extremely suspicious of police actions as a whole, but I recall some rather interesting encounters with traffic violators in which black women were the drivers, or passengers who, for whatever reason, failed to remember that they were in fact the passenger. A passenger should never speak to a police officer for the driver or attempt to control the conversation on behalf of the driver. Whether a driver or passenger, it has been my experience that people, generally, will talk themselves into receiving citations and it will usually occur within the first 30 seconds of a traffic stop when contact between the officer and the driver is initiated. As a black officer, I have experienced several interesting stops involving Black motorists. I have been asked point blank, "So, how much do they pay you to mess over other brothas?" "When are you gonna get tired of letting them use you against us?" And I've heard worse (Franklin, personal communication, 2019).

My partner and I were surveilling a residence that was suspected of drug activity. We were parked down the street, in civilian dress and in an unmarked squad car, but still identifiable as police officers if anyone took more than a glance in our direction.

Sometime during the surveillance, I spotted a vehicle drive the wrong way down a one-way street and turn down the alley where the suspect house was located. I quickly drove directly behind the vehicle and the driver immediately stopped his vehicle. The driver was a black male and the passenger a black female. I asked to see his driver's license and proof of insurance. Immediately, as the driver began to obtain the documents I requested, the female shouted in a loud voice so that there would be no mistaking the conversation she was initiating, "I think we're being racially profiled." I looked over at my partner who was standing where he should be, on the passenger side of the curbed vehicle. We both exchanged "Oh no, not THAT BS" looks at each other. After the driver gave me the required documents, I asked him, "Sir, what race are you?" He responded, "I'm black." "What race is my partner standing on the other side of your vehicle?" "He's black too." I then asked, "and what race do you think I am?" The driver studied me for about ten seconds before responding, "I think you're black too." I then told him, "well then, just who in the hell is being racially profiled here?" He gave me a look of complete shame on his face, then glared at his female passenger, who also sat there looking ashamed for having dared to have "gone there" with my partner and me. I then asked him, "why do you believe I stopped your car, sir?" "Well . . . I went the wrong way down the one-way street." As I handed back his documents to the driver (cutting him a break), I offered him some words of advice. "Don't ever allow the passenger in your vehicle to make things worse for you. If your passenger doesn't know what to say that will help you, the best thing you can tell him or her to do is to STFU." Again, the driver sat there and just glared at his female passenger (Franklin, personal communication, 2019).

Another memorable traffic stop occurred when I was a rookie patrolman, working alone on day shift. I had observed a vehicle occupied by two young black females run a stop sign. I curbed the vehicle and as I approached the driver, I asked her for her DL and proof of insurance. "My brother's the police," was her response. I again asked her to produce the documents and she responded, "I said my brother's a police officer," she said again, very dismissively. I then told her, "Well, that's nice, but I still need to see your license and your proof of insurance, miss." "Oh, you're gonna be an asshole," she then said to me as she fished for her documents in her purse. Not missing a beat, I told her, "Yes, that would be me. And I'm still waiting on your documents." At this point the driver had already talked her way into a ticket. As I walked around to the passenger side of the vehicle to obtain the information from her city vehicle license displayed on the lower part of the passenger side of the windshield, the passenger inexplicably opened her car door suddenly in an attempt to strike me with the door. I caught the door as it was about to strike me in the face. She suddenly looked very afraid, stammering out at me, "I was just gonna get out of the car, I didn't mean it!" Before I hardly knew what had occurred, I had snatched the passenger out of the car and had her in handcuffs. The driver was clearly shaken up by what her friend did. "I'm sorry about that, officer," the driver replied. As I handed the traffic citation to the driver, I told her, "Now, when you tell your cop brother what happened, don't forget to tell him that your friend was the asshole." The driver accepted her citation without further comment but did ask where her friend was going. "To lockup," I responded (Franklin, personal communication, 2019).

On another occasion I stopped a black female motorist for speeding. As I approached her vehicle, she sped off. I curbed her again, and again, as I walked up to her vehicle, she sped off. I requested backup, so the third time I curbed her I had some assisting units on the scene which caused her to cease her game of cat and mouse. After approaching the vehicle and having a brief conversation with the driver it was apparent that she was badly impaired. After getting her out of her vehicle, she said things to me that even I found shocking. Let's just say that she told me she knew I wanted to have sex with her and I should have just asked for it. She said she would have provided what she knew I needed. While I knew she was intoxicated, I was shocked at the filth that had come out of her mouth. I was furious, but I remained professional, cited her for numerous violations, and placed her in lockup, as I would any other traffic violator charged with DUI. Later in traffic court her defense counsel questioned me about what was said during the traffic stop. I was embarrassed and turned red-faced and testified to the details of the arrest. I then went into very lurid detail about what the defendant had said to me. In a short time the judge heard enough and found her guilty. I cannot recall ever stopping or arresting anyone else in my career who had said such ugly things to me, with no regard whatsoever for my position as a law enforcement professional (Franklin, personal communication, 2019).

I can't say how your average black motorist feels when being pulled over by police, but I have to assume that it is likely to be a feeling of dread overall. As adults, we are all shaped by comments made to us when we were kids by the adults in our lives, and I have to assume that few black adults tell their children positive stories from their experiences when encountering law enforcement. As former Washington, DC and Philadelphia Chief of Police, Charles Ramsey has stated law enforcement has not historically been known to be a friend to the black community in America.

Over the years I have heard many crazy things almost immediately upon approaching a motorist. The few examples I offer from experience were not a common occurrence, but all happened in some form more than once. I more than suggest none of the exclamations are ones to help a motorist's plight when pulled over for a traffic violation (Franklin, personal communication, 2019).

I have been asked the following by black traffic violators:

"Why aren't you pulling over white folks in their neighborhood?
    Oh, they told you not to do that, right?"
"Man, we just can't get a break, even from our own."
"How many brothas did they tell you to write today?

"I can't stand officers like you. You can't even see how you're being used by them."

I have been asked the following questions by white traffic violators:

"Are you an American citizen?"
"Officer, were you born here in America?"
"How did you learn to speak English so well?"
(Driver speaking in a loud voice to his passenger as I approached his window): "Well honey, he's a Puerto Rican. I guess I'm gonna get a ticket today. I just hope I can understand him" (Franklin, personal communication, 2019).

THE DIVISIONS CONTINUE ALONG
WITH POOR NATIONAL LEADERSHIP

Although we have held a limited discussion about differences between races, their thoughts, ideas and perceptions, what we believe is a major part of the divide is that races are unfamiliar with each other and some of what each race knows of the other is not well accepted. In addition, the many subcultures in each race adds more division to the debate. Generally speaking, what whites see in the media is a subculture in the black community robbing and killing. What blacks see in the media are white police officers mistreating and killing blacks. What blacks see are whites taking all the opportunities with the exclusion of blacks. What whites see are some blacks who apparently do not want to assimilate into mainstream society and do not want to educate themselves to take advantage of opportunities, but who want more handouts. Some might see these statements as exaggerations, but there are still deep racial divides in America. There certainly is a disconnect in American society between cultures, ideologies and views that is causing street demonstrations, heated arguments and the murder of police officers that, in some cases, was caused by the killing of black men by the police.

There is also a lack of national leadership. It is very clear that some Congressional Democrats and Republications have a hatred for the other's political views. This was well illustrated by the facial expressions of Nancy Pelosi, televised worldwide, during President Donald Trump's State of the Union Address in January 2018, with the same expressions displayed during the President's address in February 2019. To add fuel to the fire are statements made by President Trump that encourage racial strife. Reportedly, the president has called African nations 'sh-t holes' and 'vile' places. He has been accused of making various racially charged statements about the Koran, Mexicans and African Americans and wanting to know the ethnicity of his staff. During a civil dispute in which President Trump was a defendant, he claimed the presiding judge, who had a Hispanic surname, may be biased against him because of his Mexican heritage. Reportedly, the judge was born and raised in the state of Indiana. Notwithstanding the failures of our national leadership, there seems to be glimmers that American policing is making the effort to narrow the spread.

On October 17, 2016, Terrence M. Cunningham, President, International Association of Chiefs of Police [IACP] apologized "for the actions of the past and the role that our profession has played in society's historical mistreatment of communities of color" (Waxman 2016). On November 21, 2016, President Chuck Canterbury of the Fraternal Order of Police asked that all Americans help in reducing violence against police officers. Canterbury said, ". . . it starts with hateful speech, vile rhetoric that too often gets amplified on social media. . . . The purveyors of hate push out a product that is eagerly consumed by persons who internalize it and then act. Hateful speech can and does trigger violence and its most recent target is police officers" (Canterbury 2016). Then on November 29, 2016, Los Angeles police officials condemned a letter sent to several mosques warning "Muslims to leave the country to avoid being exterminated" (Melley, 2016).

Although American policing is making changes to their procedures through de-escalation training and changing use of force policies, there is still a need for a national movement to bridge the divide between the races and to keep civil rights concerns in the national eye.

REFERENCES

Alter, C. (2018). The young and the relentless: adults have failed to stop school shootings. now it's the kids' turn to try. *TIME* [online]. Scribd, Inc. https://www.scribd.com/article/374705530/The-Young-And-The-Relentless

American Psychological Association. (n.d.). Socioeconomic status. https://www.apa.org/topics/socioeconomic-status/index

Canterbury, C. (2016). Statement of Fraternal Order of Police national president Chuck Canterbury on recent violence against law enforcement officers. Fraternal Order of Police. https://fop.net/CmsDocument/Doc/pr_2016-1121.pdf

Center on Budget and Policy Priorities. (2017). Policy basics: where do our federal tax dollars go? Washington, DC. https://www.cbpp.org/research/federal-budget/policy-basics-where-do-our-federal-tax-dollars-go

Florida National University. (2018). What Martin Luther King Jr. accomplished for minorities. https://www.fnu.edu/martin-luther-king-jr-accomplished-minorities/

Griggs, B. (2018). Living while black: Here are all the routine activities for which police were called on African-Americans this year. *Cable News Network.* https://www.cnn.com/2018/12/20/us/living-while-black-police-calls-trnd/index.html

Hajela, D. (2018). Sympathy for white Austin bomber stirs debate about race. *PBS News Hour.* https://www.pbs.org/newshour/nation/sympathy-for-white-austin-bomber-stirs-debate-about-race

Hein, J. F. (2013). *Inside internal affairs: an in-depth look at the people, process & politics.* Flushing, NY: Looseleaf Law Publications, Inc., p. 16.

Kertscher, T. (2017). Do 90% of Americans support background checks for all gun sales? *Politifact/Wisconsin in partnership with the Journal Sentinel.* http://www.politifact.com/wisconsin/statements/2017/oct/03/chris-abele/do-90-americans-support-background-checks-all-gun-/

Kwanzaa Official Website. (2020). Nguzo Saba [Seven Principles of Kwanzaa]. http://www.officialkwanzaawebsite.org/umoja.html

Melley, B. (2016). Law enforcement condemns letters threatening Muslims. *Associated Press.* https://www.policeone.com/federal-law-enforcement/articles/244530006-Law-enforcement-condemns-letters-threatening-Muslims/?NewsletterID=244211044&utm_source=iContact&utm_medium=email&utm_content=TopNewsRight1Title&utm_campaign=P1Member&cub_id=usr_W5W3xYBArFqaU1OQ

Perkins, J. M. (2017). *Dream with me: race, love, and the struggle we must win.* Grand Rapids, MI: Baker Books.

Reuters. (2007). Chronology: who banned slavery when? https://www.reuters.com/article/uk-slavery/chronology-who-banned-slavery-when-idUSL1561464920070322

Robinson, P. H., & Robinson, S. M. (2015). *Pirates, prisoners, & lepers: lessons from life outside the law.* Potomac Books. The University of Nebraska Press.

Waxman, O. B. (2016). Police group apologizes for law enforcement's history as "face of oppression." *TIME* [online]. http://time.com/4535103/historical-mistreatment-police-chiefs-african-americans-speech/

Chapter Three

BLM ACCOMPLISHMENTS AND
POLICE RESPONSES TO BLM CRITICISM

Policemen so cherish their status as keepers of the peace and pro-
tectors of the public that they have occasionally been known to beat
to death those citizens or groups who question that status.
David Mamet, Playwright

As questionable police shootings of black men and women continue, so do the efforts of Black Lives Matter (BLM), the organization the media has seemingly placed in the vanguard of efforts for justice for all black people. Although it may be difficult to put an actual
checkmark on its achievements, it certainly can be said BLM has
raised the odds for change in not only policing but in the entire
American criminal justice system. Collectively, it is apparent BLM and
the family of like organizations have forced high level discussions on
policing actions, how and what laws should be enforced, the evident
unfairness of the judiciary and the inadequate penal system. Since the
demonstrations of 2020, the continued pressure placed on policing,
elected officials and society as a whole has caused an apparent more
rapid increase in change, but the jury is still out.

BLM organizers claim to "have ousted anti-Black politicians, won
critical legislation to benefit Black lives, and changed the terms of the
debate on Blackness around the world. Through movement and relationship building, we have also helped catalyze other movements and
shifted culture with an eye toward the dangerous impacts of anti-
Blackness" (Black Lives Matter, 2017).

According to Michael P. Jeffries, Ph.D., Associate Professor of
American Studies at Wellesley College, anti-Blackness is more than

racism, but "the debasement of black humanity, utter indifference to black suffering, and the denial of black people's right to exist" (Jeffries, 2014). To address this injustice BLM and the umbrella organization, The Movement for Black Lives, to which BLM belongs, accomplished numerous developments. These developments seem to be disjointed, some seemingly insignificant or personally self-serving, but collectively have put a face on black activism and its concerns.

THE DETERMINED FACE

In 2015, the movement's accomplishments included meeting with Democratic national candidates, black women demonstrating for recognition and respect, University of Missouri protesters causing the resignation of its president, protests being held across the country against casual racism at schools, and the black transgender community was recognized. In addition, demonstrations prompted the University of California to divest $30 million from private prison holdings, a road was named for Sandra Bland who died while in police custody, Campaign Zero was organized to protest police violence, a benefit concert was held to headline racial equality and the Police Union Contract Project was organized to determine how police union contracts fail to hold officers accountable (Workneh, 2016).

Further accomplishments were achieved in 2016 (Meyerson, 2016):

- Demands were put into words and placed on paper
  - This is in reference to the platform of The Movement for Black Lives, a group of at least 50 similar activist organizations
- Successful lawsuit against the Baton Rouge police
  - Ninety-two protestors filed suit alleging police used unconstitutional actions when demonstrating anger for the shooting of a black man. The city quickly settled with 92 plaintiffs for $100,000.
- Mothers of the Movement, mothers whose children died while interacting with police stood at the National Democratic Convention in support of Hillary Clinton.
- Former President Bill Clinton became angry.

  - At a campaign stop for his wife, Clinton became annoyed when protesters criticized his 1994 crime bill.
- Black Lives Matter attended meeting at White House
  - A meeting was held at the White House between law enforcement officials and movement members.

TAKE NOTICE

It seems black activists apparently have accomplished much more without taking full credit.

On March 23, 2012, then President Barack Obama decided to insert himself in a growing controversy over the shooting of black men and women. In the Rose Garden, during one of several meetings with activists at the White House, in an effort to recognize the unique responsibilities of being a black parent, President Obama stated, in reference to the shooting death of Trayvon Martin by George Zimmerman, "If I had a son, he'd look like Trayvon. . . . When I think of this boy, I think of my own kids" (Thompson & Wilson, 2012).

In December 2014, then President Barack Obama signed an executive order establishing the Task Force on 21st Century Policing. The task force was charged ". . . with identifying best practices and offering recommendations on how policing practices can promote effective crime reduction while building public trust" (President's Task Force, 2015).

In October 2017, through a collaborative effort by 11 American law enforcement leadership and union organizations [The] National Consensus Policy and Discussion Paper on the Use of Force was issued. The purpose of the document is to provide officers with guidelines for the use of deadly force and less-lethal force. Further consideration is given to de-escalation actions, choke holds, warning shots, firing shots at and from moving vehicles and officer training. (Coalition 2017) The warning shot policy endorsed by the coalition has caused much controversy. ". . . [The] new policy endorsing the use of warning shots by police to de-escalate potentially deadly confrontations is driving a rift among some law enforcement leaders who believe the practice only heightens risk and should be abandoned" (Johnson, 2017).

Consequently, the Chicago Police Department and reportedly many other departments, issued updated use of force guidelines. The Chicago guidelines "places sanctity of human life at [the] center of

[the] policy and emphasizes [the] overall goal of seeking voluntary compliance" (Chicago Police Department, 2017).

Over time it seems police, in general, are becoming more retrospective of their tactics but some in policing need more reflection when responding to criticism.

AMERICAN POLICING ASSISTANCE
TO THE BLACK LIVES MATTER MOVEMENT

It can also be said the final collection of accomplishments was not achieved solely by the Black Lives Matter organization or its allies, but with a certain amount of help from the American policing establishment. Some in law enforcement responded to BLM criticism with scathing remarks, while others focused on criticizing victims and their families. The black movement was further bolstered by the addition of Hollywood and music celebrities encouraged by the unwise comebacks of police representatives. The added spotlight further in-censed some in law enforcement who called for boycotts of the offending celebrity productions. Responses seem to be saying if you criticize law enforcement we will give criticism back. If you do not support law enforcement we will advocate a boycott of your livelihood.

On October 24, 2015, Quentin Tarantino participated in an anti-police rally in New York City. Commenting on his attendance at the rally, Tarantino stated, "And if you believe there's murder going on then you need to rise up and stand up against it. I'm here to say I'm on the side of the murdered" (Fox News, 2016). In response to Tarantino's appearance and statement, Patrick Lynch, president of the Patrolman's Benevolent Association said, "The police officers that Quentin Tarantino calls 'murderers' aren't living in one of his depraved big-screen fantasies—they're risking and sometimes sacrificing their lives to protect communities from real crime and mayhem" (Fox News, 2016). Tarantino attended the rally four days after a New York officer was murdered by a suspect he was pursuing. It was reported Tarantino recognized the timing of the rally was regrettable. The union called for a boycott of Tarantino's most recent film.

Offending police shootings and responses to criticism provoked Beyoncé to produce her 'Formation' video released on February 6, 2016. She also performed 'Formation' at the 2016 Super Bowl halftime show and received a bitter retort from the president of the Miami

Lodge of the Fraternal Order of Police. Javier Ortiz stated, "The fact that Beyoncé used this year's Super Bowl to divide Americans by promoting the Black Panthers and her antipolice message shows how she does not support law enforcement. . ." (Spanos, 2016). Although she denied any anti-police content, the video had a polarizing effect on many and she was forced to explain her support for police. She responded by saying much of art is misunderstood and if anyone believed she is anti-police they are mistaken. ". . . I have so much admiration and respect for officers and the families of the officers who sacrifice themselves to keep us safe. But let's be clear: I am against police brutality and injustice. Those are two separate things" (Spanos, 2016). Although a planned boycott by Miami Police to work security at a Beyoncé concert failed to materialize, the damage was done, another threatened boycott because of the criticism of police. Adding fuel to the fire were comments by Tampa, FL, Police Benevolent Association president Vinny Gericitano who stated although the union was not calling a boycott for an upcoming concert in Tampa, his membership was unhappy with Beyoncé's political views and asked that members boycott the purchase of her music and attendance at her concerts (Marrero, 2016).

On February 28, 2016, soon after the Super Bowl controversy a number of people of color boycotted the 2016 Academy Awards Ceremony because of the appearance of racial inequality, no black entertainers were nominated for an award. Comedian Chris Rock, the host, loudly voiced his misgivings of the cultural ethics of the entertainment industry. Discord lasted for weeks prior to the awards ceremony and it was impossible to hide, so Rock introduced the elephant in the room like only he could. His cutting jokes caused laughter and much thought. One of his most memorable comments was that the 'in memoriam' segment of the awards show should be devoted to 'black people who, on the way to the movies, were shot by the police.'

Anyone working in law enforcement certainly has the right to respond to criticism of their chosen profession whether they are union representatives, department leaders or members of the rank and file. However, quid pro quo or tit for tat in response to criticism fails to protect law enforcement from questionable actions. Criticism met with more criticism is irrational logic, it fuels further demonstrations and encourages closer observation. Antagonists need not provide benefit unless it is through compromise.

REFERENCES

Black Lives Matter. (2017). What we believe. https://blacklivesmatter.com/about /what-we-believe/

Chicago Police Department. (2017). General order 03-02, use of force, summary of. Chicago Police Department. https://home.chicagopolice.org/use-of-force-policy/

Coalition of 11 American Law Enforcement Leadership and Union Organizations. (2017). National consensus policy and discussion paper on the use of force. https://www.theiacp.org/resources/document/national-consensus-discussion -paper-on-use-of-force-and-consensus-policy

Fox News Entertainment and the Associated Press. (2015). NYPD union calls for boycott Quentin Tarartino films after director's anti-cop protest. http://www .foxnews.com/entertainment/2015/10/26/nypd-calls-for-boycott-quentin-tarantino -after-director-leads-anti-cop-protest.html

Jeffries, M. P., (2014). Ferguson must force us to face anti-blackness. Boston Globe. https://www.bostonglobe.com/opinion/2014/11/28/ferguson-must-force-face -anti-blackness/pKVMpGxwUYpMDyHRWPln2M/story.html

Johnson, K. (2017). Should cops be able to fire warning shots in tense situations? Even police sharply disagree. *USA Today*. https://www.usatoday.com/story /news/politics/2017/10/25/new-policy-allows-police-use-warning-shots-cops -disagree-new-policy-allowing-police-use-warning-shot/798338001/

Marrero, T. (2016). Tampa police union supports boycott of Beyoncé's music but doesn't tell members not to work her Tampa concert. *Tampa Bay Times*. http: //www.tampabay.com/news/publicsafety/will-tampa-police-officers-heed-call-to -boycott-beyonces-concert/2265915

Meyerson, C. (2016). 5 Milestone accomplishments from the year in Black Lives Matter. *Gizmodo Media Group, Splinter News*. https://splinternews.com/5-milestone -accomplishments-from-the-year-in-black-live-1793864356

President's Task Force on 21st Century Policing. (2015). *Final report of president's task force on 21st century policing*. Washington, DC: Office of Community Oriented Policing Services. https://cops.usdoj.gov/pdf/taskforce/taskforce_finalreport.pdf

Spanos, B. (2016). Beyoncé explains why 'formation' video is not anti-police. *Rolling Stone*. http://www.rollingstone.com/music/news/beyonce-businesswoman-role -burden-and-blessing-20160405

Thompson, K., & Wilson, S. (2012, March 23). Obama on Trayvon Martin: 'if I had a son, he'd look like Trayvon.' *The Washington Post*. https://www.washingtonpost .com/politics/obama-if-i-had-a-son-hed-look-like-trayvon/2012/03/23 /gIQApKPpVS_story.html

Workneh, L. (2016). 11 big accomplishments black activists achieved in 2015. *HuffPost*. https://www.huffingtonpost.com/entry/11-big-accomplishments-black -activists-achieved-in-2015_us_567996bae4b0b958f6583320

Chapter Four

MORE ABUSE—MORE DENIAL—
MORE CRITICISM—LESS RECRUITS

Gentlemen, get the thing straight once and for all—the policeman isn't there to create disorder, the policeman is there to preserve disorder.

Richard J. Daley
May of Chicago, 1955–1976

The above statement was made by 'Da Mare' to the media while defending police misconduct during the 1968 Democratic National Convention held in Chicago. Richard J. Daley, during his tenure as Chicago's mayor, was well known for malapropisms, the misuse or confusion of words. Along with the "preserve disorder" confusion, over his 21-year tenure, he reportedly also said "walking pedestrians," "alcoholics unanimous" and once told the city council parliamentarian to read a regulation for the enlightenment, edification and hallucination of the alderman. Although Mayor Daley did appoint O.W. Wilson, a leading criminologist, to lead the Chicago Police Department during most of the 1960s, Wilson had little effect on police culture. It is questionable whether police misconduct lessened during Wilson's tenure, but transgressions rose to the surface soon after Wilson's departure during the 1968 Democratic Convention. Blatant wrongdoing continued throughout the final decades of the 20th century into the 21st.

49

MORE ABUSE, A NEW AGE FOR
PROTESTS AND POLITICS AS USUAL

Remembering Commander Jon Burge of the Chicago Police Department, activists were still arguing for change when in 2010, Burge was convicted of perjury and obstruction of justice for his lead role in the torture of close to 200 mostly black suspects accused of various crimes. In 2017, the city created a $5.5 million reparation fund to compensate victims who could prove they were tortured by Burge or others. Burge reversed his usual silence and stated he found it hard to believe politicians could even think about giving reparations to "human vermin" (Spielman, 2015). To some Burge's comment seems to be right out of the 19th century and certainly gives credence to protests.

Contemporary protests are markedly different from past dissent. New age discord is expressed by highly visible entertainers and organizations with extraordinary information exchange. Law enforcement, however, continues to follow tried and true 20th century replies because, as Radley Balko states ". . . law enforcement is politically positioned in a way that basically immunizes [them] from criticism and oversight. Republicans have long been loath to criticize police and police unions. . . . Democrats have been playing defense on law-and-order issues since . . . the 1988 election. Any instinct to defend the disadvantaged groups disproportionately affected by police abuse gets drowned out by that and by the enormous influence wielded by police unions" (Balko, 2015).

Balko believes the Fraternal Order of Police, other police organizations, and law enforcement officials have an unusual stronghold on public debate. "Because they have no natural opponents in politics (the way, say, teachers unions do), and because it's so easy to stir up the fear of crime, they can marginalize their critics, claim injury at the slightest criticism, and send their critics running for cover" (Balko 2015). In a relatively short period of time, police organizations have grown powerful. At the same time critics were running for cover, significant reforms for officers were achieved by unions through litigation. Notable gains in benefits, work hours and conditions were achieved with lawsuits.

Interestingly, unions in American policing were prohibited until the mid-20th century. Prior to legalization in the 1960s, officers in the

United States had to rely on fraternal organizations and benefit associations to represent their interests. On the other hand, police unions in many European countries were legalized just prior to and soon after the first world war in the early 20th century. As unionization in the U.S. surged because of legalization, the FOP resisted affirmative action that gave rise to the Afro-American Patrolmen's League in Chicago and elsewhere (Klein, 2014). The organization not only represented the interests of black officers, but also sought justice for blacks mistreated in the justice system and for fair police services in the community (WTTW, 2016). The introduction of women into mainstream law enforcement in the early 1970s also threatened the white male dominated unions. Further resistance to diversity then led to the formation of woman's organizations and now in the 21st century LGBTQ [lesbian, gay, bisexual, transgender and queer or questioning] associations (Klein, 2014).

The fundamental, collective objective of these organizations, although in their own self-serving way, is to give a voice to officers who feel they have no control over their profession or their lives because of tyrannical superiors and politicians. Promotions, discipline, working conditions and pay scale can be corrupt and unreasonable (Klein 2014). According to the FOP website, officers in some communities in the early 20th century were obligated to work 12-hour shifts, 365 days a year (Fraternal Order of Police, n.d.). Consequently, the collective efforts of police leaders, the rank and file and especially unions to protect officers' interests and to preserve American policing culture are understandable, but troublesome.

HOW FAR DO THE PROTECTIONS GO?

There is little argument that policing is a demanding, dangerous job. Officers are confronted by citizens with little to no respect for authority, many have various mental health issues, and some give little value to human life. The proliferation of both legal and illegal weapons, split-second actions by suspicious persons and the requirement to maintain law and order in urgent circumstances can expose officers to perilous, uncertain situations. While the law enforcement sphere protects officers from government excesses and inherent dangers in policing it seems protection is also offered to officer bias, either unconscious or fully expressed, that can cause misconduct and foster corruption. In his book, *Inside Internal Affairs: An In-depth Look at the People, Process and Politics,* John F. Hein [one of the authors of this book] says, "Corruption [is] deep-seated, intentional dishonesty that can be attributed to an individual or organization. Misconduct is attributed to an individual and can be as serious as corruption, but can also be a mistake, not necessarily done purposely and where the individual has no intention of doing it again. Either can be a criminal offense or a policy violation" (Hein, 2013).

Misconduct can be a fatal mistake, a violation of law or policy, or simply a verbal, unprofessional expression. In past decades many occurrences of officer misconduct were covered up, quickly mini- mized, or unfairly adjudicated. As the growth of video devices in- creased, seemingly the disclosure of police misconduct has increased. This increased exposure has caused young activists to again question, as did past generations, the overzealous treatment by law enforcement of disadvantaged classes.

MORE DENIAL: A HISTORY

Over time, there have been periodic calls for higher ethical stan- dards for police, but human nature makes it difficult for some officers to accept the challenge. Historically, police response to criticism was denial. The 1910 International Association of Chiefs of Police (IACP) convention was rife with indignation by what members thought was unfair criticism of police use of the third degree; harsh treatment of citizens or threatening interrogations. Denial of any wrongdoing was the first response by the IACP, and after that, private security officers were blamed. Finally, the IACP members argued that "all this belongs in the past . . . and we hear of such things no more" (Walker, 1977). The third-degree dilemma was resurrected in 1931 with the publica- tion of Report 11 of the Committee on Law Observance and En- forcement. Commonly called the Wickersham Commission, it "found a widespread pattern of police abuse . . . police could be expected to deny accusations . . . the inflicting of pain, physical or mental . . . and the use of physical brutality to make arrests (Walker, 1977).

By the 1960s nothing had changed much in the culture of American policing. Denial of wrongdoing seemingly still worked and the third degree or variations of it continued. By 1968, however, police found a subculture of society to focus their wrath. Revolutionaries for radical societal change became a threat to things as they were. Police authority continued to be sacrosanct while the radicals and counter-culture flower children were difficult for police to differentiate. As one former Chicago Police officer put it, "a longhair is a longhair" (Kusch, 2004). The brutality of the Chicago Police at the 1968 Democratic Convention is deeply etched in the annals of history. As stated by Caitlin Gibson in the Washington Post, "In case you need a quick refresher: The 1968 Democratic National Convention in Chicago was an infamous, violent, unprecedented disaster. . . . The two sides clashed with mounting violence. . . . Onlookers and innocent bystanders—including reporters covering the scene and doctors attempting to offer medical help—were brutally beaten by the police, according to archival news accounts" (Gibson, 2016). The protesters "were a hybrid group . . . representing myriad issues and a wide range of philosophies, but they were united behind an encompassing cause: ending the long war in Vietnam and challenging Democratic leaders and their delegates to break with the past, create change—yes, that was the term then on every protester's lips—and remake the battered U.S. political system" (Johnson, 2008).

GROUPTHINK AND THE CODE OF SILENCE

In response to citizen hostility, a like attitude is expressed by police because of disputed policy changes, criticism of any sort by anyone, while interacting with misunderstood cultures, dealing with many minority citizens, or enforcing unpopular or contested laws. This hostility causes what the science of psychology calls groupthink. As reported by the *Psychology Today* website, "Groupthink occurs when a group values harmony and coherence over accurate analysis and critical evaluation. It causes individual members of a group to unquestioningly follow the word of the leader and it strongly discourages any disagreement with the consensus" (*Psychology Today,* n.d.).

Groupthink, consequently, causes a phenomenon called the code of silence, also known in American policing as the Blue Wall of Silence. As author John F. Hein stated in his book *Inside Internal Affairs,* The wall "is an unofficial show of unity or loyalty by officers when another is accused of misconduct. . ." (Hein, 2013). The wall also exists because of "officers' bias against management, politicians, the media, citizens, and internal affairs . . ." (Hein, 2013) and any other perceived threat.

We believe anyone has a certain code. Most youngsters have been told they should not 'tattle' on others. As they grow older, they learn not to get involved in controversy for their own good. In our professional careers we have known others who would not dial 911 to report an auto accident because they did not want to get involved. We have also questioned witnesses who denied seeing anything, who after tenacious, persistent and lawful interview techniques, finally provided reluctant testimony.

We suggest any profession has a code of silence. There are incompetent teachers because others will not report them to a supervisor while many parents have apprehension to report their displeasure. Parents merely request another teacher. Surgeon and author Dr. Marty Makary says in his book, *Unaccountable: What Hospitals Won't Tell You and How Transparency Can Revolutionize Health Care,* there are dangerous doctors practicing because of a code of silence among colleagues. There are 'Fred Flintstone' doctors practicing medicine who offer poor life-threatening medical services because they have not kept up with modern medical practices (Makary, 2012). Dr. Makary goes on to say that even his professors believed in the medical code of silence. If told of shockingly poor patient care, professors would not comment and never take action. In a profession where one's reputation is of chief importance, doctors who expose health-threatening incompetence face career damaging retaliation and ostracism (Makary, 2012).

A policing code of silence has most likely been in existence since the beginning of maintenance of order duties in the New World which evolved into the American policing model we have today. The police code of silence first became widely known because of Frank Serpico, a New York City officer who was fed up with corruption he saw firsthand for years. From experience we know that all officers do not follow a code and do, at times, report wrongdoing depending upon the violation and circumstances. Of course, there are numerous examples of misconduct/corruption that is known by others that is not reported to the proper authority. There are many examples of attempted cover-ups, more and more coming to light since the proliferation of video.

Two of the most infamous examples of the police code of silence in action can be found in the narrative about the Abner Louima sodomization in New York and the shooting of Laquan MacDonald in Chicago. Police crimes committed along with the code to protect them cause citizen discord.

REACH OUT AND TOUCH SOMEONE WENT AWRY

In his book, *To Protect and Serve: How to Fix America's Police* (2016), Norm Stamper says, "This is not a good thing—polarization never is. Yet, each 'side' seems content to talk past the other, which happens when honest conversation is confined to one's own family of interests, when any 'reaching out' to the other side takes the form of attacks." The other side has been reaching out.

On Dec 20, 2014, New York City police officers Raphael Ramos and Wenjian Liu were shot and killed by Ismaaiyl Brinsley, a black man, while sitting in their patrol car. Hours after he shot his girlfriend in the abdomen, he killed the officers. As he was approached by other officers, he killed himself. He had previously shown very strong anti-police sentiments on Instagram (Eversley, Lackey & Hughes, 2014). For his effort to abate police excesses, New York City Mayor Bill de Blasio was the recipient of the wrath of police unions for daring to criticize police violence (Graham, 2017).

On August 28, 2015, Harris County, Texas deputy sheriff Darren Goforth, while pumping gas, was shot and killed by Shannon Miles, a black man. "Prosecutors said Shannon Miles is accused of shooting Goforth in retaliation for being a law enforcement officer, and no other reason" (Eisenbaum & Cooper 2015).

On July 7, 2016, Micah Johnson, a black man, shot and killed five Dallas police officers, wounded nine others along with two civilians before he was killed by police. At the time of the shooting, police were providing security at a protest of the killing of black men by police. Johnson told negotiators he wanted to kill as many white police officers as he could (*Associated Press,* 2017).

On July 17, 2016, Gavin Long, a 29-year-old black man, shot and killed three officers and wounded three others in Baton Rouge, Louisiana. Long had previously posted internet videos inviting violence in response to the oppressive treatment of blacks by police

(*Associated Press,* 2017). Long left a suicide note: "The way the current system is set up, it protects all cops whether good or bad, right or wrong, instead of punishing bad cops and holding them accountable for their actions," Long wrote. "When good cops do try and stand up, speak out and point out the wrongs and criminal acts of a bad cop they get reprimanded, harassed, blackballed or blacklisted or all of these and more" (Litten, 2017).

Long goes on to acknowledge that his actions will be seen as "horrendous acts of violence," adding that he knows that his decision to shoot police officers will result in the deaths of good officers, "which are in the majority" (Litten, 2017).

"I must bring the same destruction that bad cops continue to inflict upon my people, upon bad cops as well as good cops," Long wrote. "My people, and the people in general will continue to strike back against all cops until we see that bad cops are no longer protected and allowed to flourish" (Litten, 2017).

On November 2, 2016, Scott Michael Greene, a white man with mental issues, shot and killed Sgt. Anthony Beminio of the Des Moines, Iowa police department and Officer Justin Martin of the Urbandale, Iowa police department (Fortin, 2017). Reportedly, Greene committed the murders because he did not like police officers.

On July 5, 2017. New York City police officer Miosotis Familia was shot in the head and killed while in a command vehicle. Shot by Alexander Bond, a black man with re-occurring mental health problems, had previously ranted anti-police rhetoric on Facebook (Graham, 2017).

The recoil because of police killings of black men is deadly on both sides but police unions continue to be unrepentant to fatal, excessive use of force. American policing seems to believe the profession is infallible, nothing done is wrong, and there is always a comeback that usually has something to do with officer safety. If there is something done that is exceptionally difficult to rationalize, there is a sudden silence. For a union to admit an officer committed a wrong seems to be an insurmountable demand. Because acknowledgment is so difficult to overcome, it appears police union aversion to criticism is a defense for which some officers paid the ultimate price. But the retorts are decreasing.

MORE CRITICISM—DO I REALLY WANT THIS JOB?

Responses by police leaders and union representatives to BLM criticism has encouraged the movement to increase their efforts to change police culture and improve police services, especially for people of color. This escalated resentment of police tactics is a "not so sudden" backlash that has developed over centuries. This displeasure first manifested in the modern era when in the 1950s Dr. Martin Luther King, Jr. became the most outspoken leader of the civil rights movement. This new bitterness has seemingly heightened the uncertainties, difficulties and danger experienced by all police officers. Active antagonism between American policing and activists can easily be associated with police recruitment problems, disputed police policy changes, and work slowdowns. Discord also created an even greater distance between police and the citizens they serve, the re-enforced resistance to criticism by officers, an increase in the code of silence and, regrettably, the murder of police officers.

The acrimony in law enforcement in many areas of the country forces many potential police recruits to think twice before taking the step to wearing the uniform. BLM and media criticism, U.S. Department of Justice reports on substandard police services, riots in Ferguson, and elsewhere, the increasing murder rate and street crime in Baltimore and other cities,* and numerous controversial shootings of black men around the country all play a role in police recruitment. In addition, entry level salaries can be as low as $9 per hour in rural areas to less than $45,000 per year in the highest cost of living areas in the country.

In the *San Diego Union-Tribune* David Garrick reported that "San Diego boosted pay [to be received over a three year period; 2018 to 2020] between 25 percent and 30 percent for the city's police officers . . . to help solve a crisis of departing officers that has lengthened response times, limited proactive policing and ballooned overtime budgets" (Garrick, 2017). A 2014 survey indicated that San Diego police officers were near the bottom of the pay scale when compared to departments from Los Angeles, Sacramento, San Francisco and the

---

*In late February 2019, the FBI reported in the latest Preliminary Semiannual Crime Statistics that overall crime declined during the first half of 2018. When compared to statistics from 2017, both violent and property crimes declined.

San Diego County Sheriff's Department. Garrick also reported that "City and police officials say such relatively low pay has prompted many officers to transfer to other law enforcement agencies with higher pay" (Garrick, 2017). Similarly, the Dallas Police Department is far behind its hiring goal for fiscal year 2018. The objective was to hire 250 recruits by the end of that year, but during the first quarter only 39 applicants had been hired. If recruitment continues at this rate, the department will be more than 37% short of their goal. Reportedly, recent public debate regarding police tactics, along with playing 'catch-up' with starting pay and a failing pension system, have made policing less attractive to some potential candidates (Hallman & Rajwani, 2018). The Dallas Police Department is losing more officers than it is recruiting.

The question many who are considering a career in law enforcement are asking: Is it worth it? As many in society are likely to be hostile to me, why should I endure irregular hours, risk injury or death, civil liability or criminal indictment for a low salary? But it might not be the young people who are doing the thinking about hazardous, unappreciated positions:

Many years ago my father told me he respected the police, although I believe he meant he respected their authority. He never told me what exactly happened but sometime during his adolescence he and several friends were roughed up by two officers. He also was raised on the near Southside of Chicago during the 1920s and 30s when the police were not known to be of high integrity or character. His first interaction with the police was when he was a young boy delivering the afternoon newspaper to a tavern. "There were always one or two paddy wagons [prisoner vans] on the side and six or eight policemen inside the tavern at the bar. They were always pretty well loaded, and it seemed they always had food slopped all over their uniforms." He once shouted at me, "No son of mine will be a copper!" After three years in the U.S. Army and a college degree I believe my father was a happy man when I began working as a deputy sheriff for the Will County Police in Joliet, Illinois, a good 40 miles from Chicago. The department enjoyed a much different and more affable reputation than did the Chicago Police (Hein, personal communication, 1980).

My father did not wish for me to become a Chicago police officer. As the first of his three sons to complete college with a bachelor's degree, he had hoped for bigger and safer avenues of employment for me. I can recall when a representative of the CPD called our house on a Friday afternoon; I was cordial and attentive as the man spoke to me on the phone. After I hung up the phone, my parents stood there, staring at me. "Who was that?" they inquired. I said, "That was the police department and they offered me a job." "Well, I know you turned them down," my father said to me in a matter-of-fact tone. "I start next Monday," I said. No one spoke. My parents just stared at each other. I could see the disappointment in my father's eyes and the fear for my life in my mother's (Franklin, personal communication, 2018).

Growing up in South Shore, the far southeast side of Chicago, I had not had much contact with police officers. Sure, some of my neighbors were cops, and I got along fine with all adults, so there were no issues there. I grew up in a religious household, no one in my family has ever been arrested, and we respected authority. But I also knew that cops were hard on black folks, especially black males in my age group, older teenagers and young twenty-somethings. One night my cousin and I were walking to my house from two blocks away. Suddenly, an unmarked car pulled up on us. It frightened both my cousin and I, and we began to run. We were caught and returned to the hood of the unmarked car. I had a mini tape recorder in my pocket; the cop who was interrogating me assumed it was not mine and asked me from where I had stolen it. I repeated to him several times that it was mine, but I don't think he ever believed me. I studied his face real hard, locking in the memory of him; eventually, we were released and allowed to go on our way. Little did I know that in a few short years, that officer who had the odor of hard booze on his breath who had interrogated me about my own property for what seemed like an eternity would eventually be the lieutenant of the tactical team to which I would be assigned as a police officer (Franklin, personal communication, 2018). Some have a calling, while others do not want to give up a questionable lifestyle.

I spoke to a friend who long held a position at the Chicago Police Training Academy and asked him if the BLM movement had any effect on the recruitment of black officers. He offered no opinion whether BLM affected hiring, but he did say that the department had small numbers of black recruits (Franklin, personal communication, 2018).

I shared my frustration with him that in my many years as a college professor teaching criminal justice courses I could not recall a single black male student who had successfully been hired and made it through the academy.

I do know, however, that the smoking of marijuana has become all too commonplace in many black communities. I once taught a black female student who impressed me with her outstanding test scores. I asked what her intentions of pursuing a law enforcement career were. I was surprised to hear that if she is offered a job in law enforcement, then and only then would she stop smoking marijuana. I told her if weed was that important in her life not to bother applying for a job in policing.

I also believe police misconduct against black males is having a negative effect on recruitment. I have already mentioned the bigotry I and other black males experienced in the police academy in the early 1980s. As other potential recruits are wondering if they want the grief and uncertainty of working as an officer, many blacks are also wondering if they want to enter a profession with so much animosity already built into the job against the black community (Franklin, personal communication, 2018).

My friend and I agreed another factor in recruitment of blacks is the fact many young men and women in the black community have uninvolved parents. I have lost count how many times while writing a missing persons' report I was told by parents that they do not know any of their child's friends (Franklin, personal communication, 2018).

As many people understand, serving in law enforcement is a calling for many and merely a job for others. Even though authors Franklin and Hein were cautioned, as still many are, the desire to serve can overcome the thought of probable adverse consequences.

Because of human nature, differing ideologies and poor training some questionable interactions between police and citizens will always be present which can cause deadly responses. There can also be consequences if ideologies and tactics cause confusion between domestic civil disorder and terrorist acts.

REFERENCES

Associated Press. (2017). A list of police ambush killings in the U.S., its territories. *Fox News.* https://www.foxnews.com/us/a-list-of-police-ambush-killings-in-the-us -its-territories

Balko, R. (2015). The increasing isolation of America's police. *The Washington Post.* https://www.washingtonpost.com/news/the-watch/wp/2015/05/11/the-increasing -isolation-of-americas-police/ ?utm_term=.37f5cca6ee80

Eisenbaum, J., & Cooper, N. (2015). Motive revealed in deadly shooting of Deputy Darren Goforth. *Click2Houston.com.* https://www.click2houston.com/news /motive-revealed-in-deadly-shooting-of-deputy-darren-goforth

Eversley, M., Lackey, K. & Hughes, T. (2014). 2 NYPD officers killed in ambush style shooting. *USA Today.* https://www.usatoday.com/story/news/nation/2014 /12/20/new-york-city-police-officers-shot/20698679/

Fortin, J. (2017, May 19). Iowa man is sentenced to 2 life terms in killings of 2 offi- cers. *The New York Times.* https://www.nytimes.com/2017/05/19/us/scott -michael-greene-iowa.html

Fraternal Order of Police. (n.d.). A history of the Fraternal Order of Police. https: //www.fop.net/CmsPage.aspx?id=13

Garrick, D. (2017). San Diego boosts police pay up to 30 percent amid staffing cri- sis. *The San Diego Union-Tribune.* http://www.sandiegouniontribune.com/news / politics/sd-me-police-raises-20171205-story.html

Gibson, C. (2016, July 18). What happened in Chicago in 1968, and why is every- one talking about it now? *The Washington Post.* https://www.washingtonpost .com/news/arts-and-entertainment/wp/2016/07/18/what-happened-in-chicago -in-1968-and-why-is-everyone-talking-about-it-now/?utm_term=.9008e6100063

Graham, D. A. (2017). The murder of Miosotis Familia. *The Atlantic Daily.* https: //www.theatlantic.com/news/archive/2017/07/the-murder-of-miosotis-familia /532707/

Hallman, T., & Rajwani, N. (2018, January 29). Dallas Police Department hiring lags as firefighting hiring surges. Dallas, TX: *The Dallas Morning News.* https: //www.dallasnews.com/news/dallas-city-hall/2018/01/29/dallas-police-department -hiring-lags-firefighter-hiring-surges

Hein, J. F. (1980). *Education: A way of changing the police image.* University Park, IL: Governor's State University, pp. 174–175.

Hein, J. F. 2013. *Inside internal affairs: An in-depth look at the people, process & politics.* Flushing, NY: Looseleaf Law Publications, Inc., p. 16.

Johnson, H. (2008). 1968 Democratic Convention: The bosses strike back. *Smith- sonian Magazine.* https://www.smithsonianmag.com/history/1968-democratic -convention-931079/

Klein, J. (2014). History of police unions. *Encyclopedia of criminology and criminal jus- tice,* pp. 2207–2217. https://doi.org/10.1007/978-1-4614-5690-2_463

Kusch, F. (2004). *Battleground Chicago: The police and the 1968 Democratic National Convention.* Chicago: University of Chicago Press.

Litten, K. (2017, June 30). Read the suicide note left by Baton Rouge police shoot- er Gavin Long. New Orleans, LA: *The Times-Picayune.* http://www.nola.com /politics/index.ssf/2017/06/baton_rouge_police_shooting_2.html

Makary, M. (2012). *Unaccountable: What hospitals won't tell you and how transparency can revolutionize health care.* New York, NY: Bloomsbury Press, pp. 17–57.

Psychology Today. (n.d.). What is groupthink? Sussex Publishers, LLC. https://www.psychologytoday.com/basics/groupthink

Spielman, F. (2015). Disgraced Chicago cop Jon Burge breaks silence, condemns $5.5 million reparations fund. Chicago, IL: *Chicago Sun-Times.* https://chicago .suntimes.com/2015/4/17/18469974/disgraced-chicago-cop-jon-burge-breaks -silence-condemns-5-5-million-reparations-fund

Stamper, N. (2016). *To protect and serve: How to fix America's police.* New York, NY: Nations Books, p. xviii.

Walker, S. (1977). *A critical history of police reform: The emergence of professionalism.* Lexington, MA: D.C. Heath & Co., pp. 25–58.

WTTW Public Broadcasting digital archives. (2016). *Power, politics, & pride: Afro-American Patrolmen's League.* https://interactive.wttw.com/dusable-to-obama/afro -american-patrolmens-league

Chapter Five

CRIME V. TERRORISM
AND THE USE OF FORCE

All terrorist acts are criminal acts, not all criminal acts are terrorism. A violent civil disturbance is not terrorism.

Franklin and Hein

It seems American policing is beginning to understand overly aggressive enforcement or military style actions to address civil discord are counterproductive for both citizens and the police. This fact might be another accomplishment that could be credited to the BLM movement.

Community rather than overly aggressive, hurtful policing is a better way to maintain order. However, the human element has a way of impeding quality service. Criminal conduct, disrespect, fear, mental illness to include PTSD, bias, poor training and absent or unconcerned supervisors all contribute to a poor policing model. Too often aggressive policing causes unwise citizen interactions that frequently conclude with the use of force, many times in excess. This contact, along with an officer's mindset of authority with immediate and unquestioned compliance often has deadly consequences.

Failed policing practices have been exasperated by the increase of 20th century police militarism and 21st century actions against terrorism. An increasing violent society along with American law enforcement joining the fight against international terrorism has caused a confusion between crime and terror. Crime is usually defined as a violation of man's law that is a prohibition of actions, whether a felony or misdemeanor which has been traditionally addressed by American policing. According to 18 United States Code 2331, international terrorism is a federal crime when a conspiracy to kill occurs, an attempt is made to kill or the death of a U.S. citizen occurs primarily *outside* of the United States that is a violation of U.S. criminal laws or would be a criminal violation if committed within U.S. jurisdiction. Domestic terrorism is defined the same, but the violation would primarily occur *inside* the boundaries of the United States and its territories. Both international and domestic terrorism are also defined as intended to intimidate or coerce a civilian population; to influence the policy of a government by intimidation or coercion; or to affect the conduct of a government by mass destruction, assassination or kidnapping. Terrorism violations are federally prosecuted by using appropriate federal laws like violations against murder, bombing and harming interstate and foreign commerce. Whether international or domestic, terrorism is a crime committed because of ideology, not a crime known usually to be addressed by local police. Both international and domestic terrorism are FBI priorities, but the local police can take a role in both types of investigations depending upon the circumstances. In fact, local policing often is the eyes and ears of federal policing. Violations of domestic terrorism can be prosecuted in federal or state courts depending upon the circumstances. Because of the federal/local cooperation and the military mindset of some local police officials, law enforcement can confuse well known battlefield counterterrorism tactics used to suppress international terrorism with the restraint of citizen discord.

As we stated, the difference between what we will call traditional crime and terrorism is that terrorism is fueled by an ideology. Traditional crime has many causes while terrorism is sustained by beliefs of superiority leading to attempts of forced social change. Terrorism may use military style tactics to gain advantage, to force a change in behavior. A terrorist uses violence or non-violence as intimidation to have a social influence. Military tactics and force must be opposed with military tactics and force until more civil tactics are accepted. These same tactics should not be employed to address civil discord where dissatisfaction with life, not ideology, is the catalyst.

DIFFICULTY FINDING THE 'SWEET SPOT'

A military model of policing has been present since Sir Robert Peel first presented the idea of a modern, organized police service in

London, England in 1829. American policing soon followed Peel's model with various command and rank structures, uniforms, insignia and regulations just as do military units. However, in the last 50 years, American policing has gone beyond being a military model and conceivably became a civil military service.

According to Radley Balko, "There's now a dominant military culture within modern police agencies" (Balko, 2013). Many vendors of products marketed to police departments "sell the same products to both the military and civilian police agencies. . . . They use war imagery to ply their goods because that's what makes cops and police departments want to buy them" (Balko, 2013).

Some jurisdictions are more aggressive than others, but Special Weapons and Tactics teams (S.W.A.T.), with the help of federal grants and get tough on crime politicians, have become an invading force in many areas. Riots and the proliferation of the drug culture in the 20th century and terrorism in the 21st century have all provided fuel for a number of police departments to join in the militarization of police service. Over the years S.W.A.T. has performed some needed actions to keep citizens and police officers safe. However, at the same time S.W.A.T. type actions have made an uncounted number of numbing mistakes like entering the wrong house. Teams have killed animals, innocent people and other members of S.W.A.T. teams. Some teams are used for regulatory and misdemeanor actions, all while wearing military garb and carrying assault weapons (Balko, 2013) Strong enforcement advocates would say a changing society and globalization have made the militarization of policing a necessity. Critics would say militarization has broadened the distance between the police and citizens served. Critics also say that militarization has made a mockery of the Fourth Amendment to the U.S. Constitution that ensures a person has the right to privacy in their homes and freedom from unreasonable searches and seizures.

Because of failed responses to riots, especially in Ferguson, some departments are re-evaluating their command presence and military type actions at demonstrations. An example is the Charlottesville, Virginia response to a white nationalist rally in August 2017. It seems Charlottesville is an illustration of a sorely inadequate response, while Ferguson might be considered an example of a response showing too much force. What appears to be happening, if serious retrospective analysis continues, is that BLM may have stimulated some to take a look at the age-old tried but failed manner in which police engage demonstrators. The failure of police in Charlottesville, both city and state, to adequately protect the fundamental rights of citizens has caused some to show a deep-seated distrust of government (CBS News, 2017). Apparently this distrust is by conservative, stay tough on crime citizens who wanted a strong show of force, while there is another faction of liberals who distrust government because they advocate a more balanced approach. It is yet to be determined whether the insufficient response was from poor planning or the fact authorities were reluctant to show force, the force amply demonstrated in Ferguson.

What Charlottesville may have been attempting is to find a "sweet spot," or their utility—utility being the department's quality of being useful. Utility can also represent the satisfaction expressed by citizens served or protected during a police action. It can also mean the success or failure of services, or criticism or praise by others. The 21st century response to a crime, however, must be appropriate just as punishment for felonies and misdemeanors are appropriate to any offense.

TERRORISM IS A FELONY

A felony is usually defined as a crime that is punishable by imprisonment for more than one year. It is a more serious crime than one which is a misdemeanor, a crime punishable for one year or less. A felony can be violent or non-violent like any number of terrorist acts; violent like a murder or non-violent like an Internet virus. Another type of felony is treason that is a violation of allegiance to the United States. An American citizen can be treasonous by becoming a terrorist and committing or attempting to commit an act of terror. For any crime, whether a felony or misdemeanor, there are certain elements of proof that must be present to show a crime was committed. Different crimes can have different elements of proof. Various elements can be willfulness, knowledge and intent. Elements include the proof that an accused acted deliberately with knowledge without mistake, voluntarily with specific intent to commit an illegal act.

EYE FOR EYE, TOOTH FOR TOOTH

Elements certainly have changed since the creation of the Code of Hammurabi. Hammurabi was the ruler of Babylon who developed the code to control Mesopotamian society sometime circa 1800-1750 B.C. He is infamous for the law, "Eye for eye, tooth for tooth." "The codes have served as a model for establishing justice in other cultures . . . [but the code] . . . is not a complete set of laws, but more a series of enactments addressing specific cases and subjects. . . ." (Biography.com, n.d.). Some of the more interesting rules in the code are burglars will be put to death along with anyone who receives stolen property, a wife who has not been discreet and has belittled her husband will be drowned, and a son who strikes his father will have his hand cut off (Wright State University, n.d.).

Advancing to a fairer, more reasonable and just era, crime and crimes of terror are still high on the minds of many. There are no known statistics on the crime rate in Mesopotamia, but it is doubted the likelihood of death, drowning or amputation stopped some from stealing, adultery or assault, but there are three excuses for crime: passion, opportunity and premeditation.

CRIME OF PASSION

A crime of passion is usually a violent crime; it can be a terrorist act, assault or homicide, but it can also include the destruction of an inanimate object, a thing of value. The person who commits the act usually does it in a sudden fit of anger because of a bitterness, heartbreak, animosity, an escalation of resentment, despair because of love, hate, failure, frustration and a number of other things such as shown in the two cases that follow:

Clara Harris, a Houston, TX, dentist was granted parole after serving 15 years of a 20 year sentence. She was sentenced in 2002 for first degree murder. In a sudden fit of rage she ran over her husband with her Mercedes-Benz three times when she determined he was having an affair with a former employee. (Burke, 2017)

The murder of Nicole Brown Simpson, the ex-wife of O.J. Simpson, and a restaurant worker, Ronald Goldman, in June 1994, was a crime of passion. Reportedly, Nicole Simpson was nearly decapitated by knife wounds—a sure sign of passion. Although O.J. Simpson was acquitted of murder charges he was later found civilly liable for the deaths. The not guilty verdict of Simpson had staggering racial overtones when announced in 1995. Much of black America initially read the verdict as a cause for celebration—that the system that advantages the wealthy and the white had, in this instance, set a very rich black man free. For white Americans, some of whom were no doubt less familiar with or at least personally affected by a criminal justice system that today is increasingly viewed as less fair to African Americans, Simpson was just a wealthy and abusive black man who might have gotten away with murder. (Ross, 2016)

For a crime of passion to be a terrorist act there must be the inclusion of an ideology for social change. There must be the desire of radical government or social reordering. Obviously, the murder of a husband or wife does not fit a terrorist act, but a terrorist act can be a crime of passion because of compelling emotion.

CRIME OF OPPORTUNITY

A crime of opportunity can be violent or non-violent: armed robbery, shoplifting or a terrorist act. One who commits this crime simply sees a chance to obtain something of value and seizes the moment. The something of value for a terrorist act is intimidation of citizens. The act is committed with little to no thought; there is no premeditation. Premeditation does not include, 'Hey, let's go boost some unlocked cars.' Some criminalists believe if criminals gave some thought to what they were about to do they may not commit a violent crime. Others believe a criminal makes rational choices and looks for a big haul with little exertion or jeopardy. An example of a crime of opportunity can be an unlocked vehicle. Reckless teenagers with sticky fingers have been known to burglarize a vehicle that was left unlocked.

In recent months, citizens of Wilton Manors, Florida have seen a spike in car burglaries. Video surveillance systems have recorded the offenders in action. The recordings revealed that the culprits walked from car to car, checking to see if the doors were locked. In each instance, if the car doors were locked, they simply moved on to the next car. They did not break the windows, as doing so would have drawn attention to them. When an unlocked automobile was discovered, the criminal searched through the car and stole what they could. He or she then proceeded to the next vehicle in search of more unlocked doors and more items to steal (City of Wilton Manors, Florida, n.d.).

Boosting a car is obviously not an act of terror, but terrorism can be a crime of opportunity for a group or individual to act on a call of jihad. Many calls for jihad, a sacred duty of holy war believed by some Muslims, have been voiced in recent years. A jihad may give many the signal to look for a quick chance to cause death and destruction, to intimidate noncombatant citizens in an effort to force social change.

CRIME OF PREMEDITATION

A crime of premeditation is loaded with intent and sometimes, just like a crime of passion, can be charged with emotion. One who commits a premeditated crime shows intent because of the planning, the effort to execute the undertaking, and the preparation needed to complete the task. Premeditation can show persistence. Although there can be much thought put into a premeditated crime, determining one's other options, apparently, is not part of the process.

- "Philadelphia Police and the FBI are investigating an armored car heist in Tacony in which two armed robbers made off with $105,000. . . . It appears to have been a well-coordinated heist, and at this point, the robbers are still on the run" (ABC Action News, 2018).
- "Metro Nashville Police arrested suspected serial bank robber Jason Phillip Xenos, 32, on Saturday evening. . . . Police say Xenos is suspected to have robbed three banks in Nashville and one in Smyrna, all by passing notes to a teller" (WSMV-TV News, 2017).

Robbing a bank or armored car might be considered a higher level, certainly more sophisticated crime than that of burglarizing a vehicle but are not acts of terror. However, we are sure there is no

argument that acts of terror, acts to force social change, are predomi-
nately crimes of premeditation.

Remember, all terrorist acts are criminal acts, but not all criminal
acts are terrorism; a violent civil disturbance is not terrorism. A
response to a civil disorder, even when transitioned into riotous criminal acts, cannot be addressed with a response more suited to a terrorist attack.

WHAT CREATES A CRIMINAL

The discussion of crime and knowing the fact it has been taking
place since the beginning of time makes one wonder what creates a
criminal? We make a distinction between an international or domestic criminal terrorist who is a zealot of an extreme ideology usually
addressed by U.S. federal or military authorities and a criminal usually addressed by local police. Pundits continue to argue what creates a
terrorist zealot and, in fact, still debate what causes a traditional criminal. For our purposes, we will limit our discussion to factors which
might create a traditional criminal.

According to Regis University School of Contemporary Liberal
Studies, "In criminology and the study of behaviors, we talk about
risks and contributing factors rather than causes. If Joey was raised by
absent parents, in a low-income neighborhood and was a victim of
violent crime that is not guaranteed to cause him to become a violent
criminal as an adult. However, those factors increase his risk factors
for becoming an adult criminal. Behavioral scientists study these factors so that social workers, school counselors and family therapists
may learn to recognize the risks and intervene early" (Regis
University, n.d.). But no theory among many has ever clearly
answered the question: what makes a violent criminal?

According to Youth Violence: A Report of the Surgeon General,
normal development of children and adolescents open to violence can
be disruptive causing serious consequences on their mental, physical,
and emotional health. Additional studies submit that children learn
violent behavior by observing their parents. Attachment to parents
which might be a protective factor can have an opposite effect if the
parents are violent or exhibit criminal propensity. There are various
theories why violence begins in adolescence, but violence can in-

crease in the teen years. Environmental and biological factors, the interaction with others and emotional changes can be risk factors for violent behavior (Office of the Surgeon General, n.d.).

A police officer working in a criminal environment does not need to read a complex academic theory brimming with statistical analyses to know children, adolescents and adults who have an inclination for crime or a strong disrespect for authority learned their attitudes, behaviors, values, beliefs and perceptions from others in their daily environment. These factors along with mental issues found in any society can ignite interactions with police authority with tumultuous results.

HEY FOOL, YOUR ACTIONS ARE BEING RECORDED!

These tumultuous results have been ongoing for centuries but with the advent and proliferation of video recordings of police interactions with citizens, the recognition of violent results are increasing. While some would agree with increasing results, others would say there has always been a brutish or coarse police culture that promotes insolence. The crude culture responded to this self-produced acrimony with more boorish confrontations many with the use of force. There are some who exhibit enthusiasm that technology advances will bring order to officer conduct and decrease instances of excessive use of force.

Video technology means someone just might be watching and recording an officer's conduct. But not all officers seem to understand that they may be under surveillance. Not until recently has history documented controversy regarding recording the actions of police officers. In many cities and states . . . it [was] illegal for a citizen to video police in action and arrests [when] made (Hein, 2013). However, on July 7, 2017, a federal appeals court in Philadelphia ruled "Americans have a constitutional right to film on-duty police officers in public. . . . In its decision in *Fields v. City of Philadelphia* [No. 16-1650], the Third Circuit Court of Appeals said the First Amendment's protections extended to two people who used their smartphones to record police interactions with a third party. . . . The First, Fifth, Seventh, Ninth, and Eleventh Circuits have also issued similar rulings, starting in 2011, to protect bystanders who record police actions. Their collective jurisdictions now amount to exactly half of U.S. states and roughly 60 percent of the American population. No federal appeals court has ruled to the contrary; the Supreme Court has not weighed in on the subject" (Ford, 2017). Videos have become a big part in citizen efforts to challenge police misconduct and excessive use of force.

COVERING YOUR BUTT AND THE USE OF FORCE

Police use of force has a long history of debate. What amount of force should be used and for what reason? This debate was addressed in a collaborative effort by a number of organizations. The National Consensus Policy and Discussion Paper on the Use of Force, a collaborative effort of 11 law enforcement leadership and labor organizations, was published in October 2017. The new consensus is that:

> Officers shall use only the force that is objectively reasonable to effectively bring an incident under control, while protecting the safety of the officer and others. Officers shall use force only when no reasonably effective alternative appears to exist and shall use only the level of force which a reasonably prudent officer would use under the same or similar circumstances. . . . The decision to use force "requires careful attention to the facts and circumstances of each particular case, including the severity of the crime at issue, whether the suspect poses an immediate threat to the safety of the officer or others, and whether he is actively resisting arrest or attempting to evade arrest by flight. (Association of State Criminal Investigative Agencies et al., 2017)

To cover the bases for legal liability, the paper goes on to say, as sited in Graham v. Connor, 490 U.S. 386 (1989), "In addition, "the 'reasonableness' of a particular use of force must be judged from the perspective of a reasonable officer on the scene, rather than with the 20/20 vision of hindsight . . . the question is whether the officers' actions are 'objectively reasonable' in light of the facts and circumstances confronting them" (Clark, 2014).

Graham v. Conner, 490 U.S. 386 (1989) was a United States Supreme Court decision in which the Court determined "an officer must apply constitutionally appropriate levels of force, based on the unique circumstances of each case. The officer's force should be applied in the same basic way that an 'objectively reasonable' officer would in the same circumstances. The Supreme Court has repeatedly said that the most important factor to consider in applying force is the threat faced by the officer or others at the scene" (Bloom, 2005).

Along with the expanding use of video, it seems textbook answers to street misconduct did not always mitigate gross violations of policy. One train of thought suggests officer attitudes must change from one of a military mindset to one of protector or guardian. The military mindset has been growing since the infancy of S.W.A.T in the 1960s and the warrior mindset has exploded since the terror attacks of September 11, 2001. An opposing thought suggests a military mindset is a mentality that is needed in the 21st century to address domestic turmoil and terrorist threats. Terrorism is a crime that any officer in the United States should have a working knowledge of, but terrorism is more than what most people suspect.

TERRORISM IS MORE THAN AN EXPLOSION

If members of the American public were asked the history of terrorism, many would know little prior to the September 11, 2001, attacks. In fact, terrorism was first thought to be used as a tool of change in Roman times. Mia Bloom, in her book, *Dying to Kill: The Allure of Suicide Terrorism,* reports methods of the Thugs of India, circa 650 B.C., as another example of terrorism. They strangled their victims as an affront to orthodox Hinduism (Bloom, 2005). However, Mark LeVine reports, "The first recorded use of 'terrorism' and 'terrorist' was in 1795, relating to the Reign of Terror instituted by the French government. The use of 'terrorist' to signify anti-government activities was recorded in 1866 referring to Ireland, and in 1883 referring to Russia" (LeVine, 2001).

Terrorism can be difficult to define because as the quip goes, 'one man's terrorist, is another man's freedom fighter.' During the American Revolution many colonialists could have been considered terrorists by the British Army. During the American Civil War, William Tecumseh Sherman could have been considered a terrorist by southern citizens who endured the March to the Sea. Osama Bin Laden was once considered a freedom fighter after the invasion of Afghanistan by the Soviet Army.

Among hundreds of definitions, the U.S. Government's definition of terrorism, Title 18 U.S. Code, subsection 2331(5): "the term domestic terrorism means activities that: (A) involve acts dangerous to human life that are a violation of the criminal laws of the United States or of any State; (B) appear to be intended (i) to intimidate or coerce a civilian population, (ii) to influence the policy of a government by intimidation or coercion, or (iii) to affect the conduct of a government by mass destruction, assassination, or kidnapping, and (C) occur primarily within the territorial jurisdiction of the United States. More specifically, the FBI defines terrorism as a crime "perpetrated by individuals and/or groups inspired by or associated with primarily U.S.-based movements that espouse extremist ideologies of a political, religious, social, racial, or environmental nature" (FBI, 2018). There are similar but appropriate definitions for international terrorism.

Terrorism, whether domestic or international, is committed to instill fear in others to compel influence, but it is not necessarily a bomb, or a passenger jet loaded with fuel flown into a building or a truck careening down a busy avenue before plowing into people to kill as many as possible. Terrorism can take many forms in an attempt to intimidate a country or entity by placing citizen safety in jeopardy. To influence a government, or even a corporation, an attack could be introducing a disease through the U.S. Mail or an attack through the Internet that causes the interruption of Wall Street financial institutions. An attack could be made by individuals who control a U.S. based foreign company to interrupt the manufacture of a product essential to U.S. national security. Any event detrimental to the U.S. economy could be used to influence the U.S. Government, to instill fear in citizens to disrupt normal life or change a way of life or way of thinking. As two Chinese military officials wrote in "Unrestricted Warfare" regarding the overwhelming victory by U.S. led forces in the 1991 Gulf War, competing governments have learned a direct military confrontation with the United States is futile, a war by others means is necessary. Those other means include financial and technological resources. The Internet and economic warfare would be used to place the opponent at a disadvantage so direct military action would not be necessary (Liang & Xiangsui, 1999). Terrorism is a criminal act to influence a government, a corporation or the lives of citizens. Terrorist acts should not be confused with traditional criminal acts committed because of an opportunity, a passion, a careless thought, or because of frustration.

RIOTERS AND STREET THUGS ARE NOT TERRORISTS

An inner-city gang of criminals might use intimidation and fear to collect protection money, but it is a street crime, not an act of terrorism. Some criminology students will confuse street crime with terrorist acts. That might be because they have come face to face with an act "to intimidate or coerce a civilian population," but for a gang-related street crime to be categorized as terrorism, as the FBI more than suggests, the crime must be associated with "extremist ideologies" that present-day terrorism associates with political or religious beliefs beyond social norms.

A conflict was created in American law enforcement that has confused the lines that should be drawn between the interdiction of terrorism and the tactics used to keep the peace and maintain order. As already discussed, the militarization of policing has continued or may have increased the divide between officers and some citizens. Since the 1960s, S.W.A.T has taken a greater role in protecting officers but has increased constitutional violations. Since 1990, the federal government has administered and promoted the 1033 program, administered by the Law Enforcement Support Office, more commonly called the LESO Program. The program transfers excess military equipment and supplies to American law enforcement agencies. Since 1990, agencies have taken possession of non-lethal items like winter clothing, flashlights and medical supplies, but also various lethal items usually saved for the battlefield like tracked vehicles, bayonets, grenade launchers and .50 caliber machine guns.

As Radley Balko reported in the *Huffington Post* in June 2012, "The [LESO] program has also given out weapons that have been deemed, at times, inappropriate for war situations, let alone being unnecessary for a domestic police force. Several counties, including Maricopa County, Arizona and Richland County, South Carolina, have acquired tanks with belt-fed, 360-degree rotating machine gun turrets that shoot .50 caliber ammunition. A .50 caliber bullet is powerful enough to cut through several city blocks and any buildings that may be in its way. Richland County Sheriff Leon Lott sent out a press release shortly after acquiring his tank in 2008 announcing he had named the weapon "The Peacemaker" (Balko, 2012).

The authors' curiosity peaked when we read the Richland County Sheriff may have received and still may have a .50 caliber machine gun. We had already discovered the 'tank' was actually an armored personnel carrier that are two different military vehicles—one a formidable war machine, the other a useful vehicle for police protection. Two phone calls and one email message to the sheriff's office and not a word of confirmation or denial about the machine gun. We find this lack of communication puzzling, since in January 2018 the Richland County Sheriff's Department became the first sheriff's department in the United States to place the words 'PEACE OFFICER' on its fleet of patrol cars (Franklin & Hein, 2019).

Many have asked: how will a .50 caliber machine gun be used to maintain order in the United States? On January 16, 2015, then President Barack Obama issued executive order 13688, regarding federal support for local law enforcement acquisition to establish an interagency Law Enforcement Working Group to: 1) identify agency action that can improve federal support for the acquisition of controlled [military] equipment; 2) provide law enforcement agencies with controlled [military] equipment that is appropriate to the needs of their community; 3) ensure proper training to employ the equipment; 4) ensure operational practices and standards are adopted to prevent the misuse or abuse of the controlled [military] equipment; and 5) ensure that compliance with civil rights requirements are followed (White House executive order, 2015).

In May 2015, then President Barack Obama, acting upon the working group's recommendations, banned various types of military equipment following far-reaching criticism for a military-like response to public disorder in Ferguson in the summer of 2014. As President Obama said, "We've seen how militarized gear can sometimes give people a feeling like they're [the police] an occupying force, as opposed to a force that's part of the community that's protecting them and serving them . . . [military equipment can] alienate and intimidate local residents and may send the wrong message" (Korte, 2015). The wrong message was displayed in the city of Ferguson, Missouri.

Doug Wyllie, PoliceOne.com Senior Contributor says, "It's also not surprising that the types of equipment now being banned from police use are arbitrary: (sic) Camouflage clothing looks scary to people who don't understand its usefulness in not getting shot when you are looking for bad guys like Eric Fran or Chris Dorner, for example" (Wyllie, 2015).

Eric Frain is a self-taught survivalist who killed one Pennsylvania State Trooper and wounded another in September 2014. Nearly one thousand officers from local, state and federal agencies hunted for Frain who hid in rural areas for over 1 1/2 months before his capture (Franklin & Hein 2019).

Chris Dorner, a former LAPD officer fired for making false statements, posted on Facebook his intentions of waging war against the LAPD and their families unless the department publicly admitted he was retaliated against for reporting the excessive use of force by his partner. He began shooting police officers and civilians in random attacks, killing four and wounding three. For over a week, officers all over southern California looked for Dorner who was eventually killed during a standoff with officers in a mountainous area (Franklin & Hein 2019).

WILL IT BE KABUL OR MAYBERRY?

Some military equipment and clothing is useful. The safety of officers is of utmost importance. It is also useful to know and important to understand the United States should not be treated, outfitted, or thought of as a war zone. Is it necessary for police officers to wear camouflage clothing in an urban area and be armed with automatic assault rifles when keeping the peace when no known threat is apparent?

In August 2017, newly elected President Donald Trump reversed the Obama limitations. "Police departments will now have access to military surplus equipment typically used in warfare, including grenade launchers, armored vehicles and bayonets, Attorney General Jeff Sessions announced on Monday, describing it as "lifesaving gear"" (Goldman, 2017).

In the summer of 2015, however, the engines of war were not needed in the state of Maryland, but a sense of understanding was. Reported in the *Baltimore Sun,* "Baltimore's recent unrest wasn't quelled by trotting out .50 caliber machine guns. It didn't involve grenade launchers of any kind, nor was peace restored by a phalanx of police armored vehicles in the middle of Sandtown-Winchester. Ultimately, the week-long public disturbance was curtailed by following fairly standard police crowd control efforts (including exercising considerable restraint at times) and the willingness of elected officials to acknowledge protestor's concerns—and take action—regarding the death of Freddie Gray" (Baltimore Sun, 2015).

Now we know there are options other than the use of force to quell confrontations when, seemingly, neither of the opposing sides is listening. Are American policing spokespersons listening when told citizens do not want Ferguson, Baltimore or Mayberry to look like Kabul? Or are those spokespersons still defensive against perceived criticisms against police actions? Some inside and out of American policing, however, are taking steps, albeit small, to reexamine policies, procedures, training, education and expectations to correct past errors and promote better service.

REFERENCES

ABC Action News. (2018). $105,000 taken in armored car heist outside bank in Tacony. Philadelphia, PA. http://6abc.com/news/heist-investigation-leads-to-roxborough apartment/29627/

Association of State Criminal Investigative Agencies et al. (2017). National consensus policy and discussion paper on the use of force. https://www.theiacp.org/resources/document/national-consensus-discussion-paperon-use-of-force-and-consensus-policy

Balko, R. (2012). Pentagon suspends program that gives military weapons to cops. *HuffPost.* https://www.huffpost.com/entry/pentagon-suspends-weapons-program-cops-military_n_1585328

Balko, R. (2013). *Rise of the warrior cop.* New York, NY: Public Affairs/Perseus Books Group, p. xii.

Baltimore Sun, The. (2015). Police won't miss grenade launchers. Editorial. https://www.baltimoresun.com/opinion/editorial/bs-ed-military-20150519story.html

Biography.com. (n.d.). Hammurabi. https://www.biography.com/people/hammurabi-9327033

Bloom, M. (2005). *Dying to kill: the allure of suicide terrorism.* New York, NY: Columbia University Press, pp. 5–6.

Burke, M. (2017). Dentist who fatally ran over husband after learning about his affairs granted parole. *New York Daily News.* https://www.nydailynews.com/news/crime/dentist-killed-husband-car-affair-granted-parole-article-1.3617302

CBS News. (2017). Charlottesville protest report finds police failed at violent rally. https://www.cbsnews.com/news/charlottesville-protest-report-police-failed-violent-rally/#

City of Wilton Manors, Florida. (n.d). Auto burglary is a crime of opportunity. Automobile Burglary Prevention Tips. https://www.wiltonmanors.com/301/Auto-Burglaries

Clark, M. (2014). Understanding Graham v. Connor. *Police: The Law Enforcement Magazine.* https://www.policemag.com/341717/understanding-graham-v-connor

Federal Bureau of Investigation. (2018). What We Investigate: Terrorism. https://www.fbi.gov/investigate/terrorism

Ford, M. (2017). A major victory for the right to record police. *The Atlantic*. https://www.theatlantic.com/politics/archive/2017/07/a-major-victory-for-the -right-to-record-police/533031/

Goldman, A. (2017). Trump reverses restrictions on military hardware for police. *The New York Times*. https://www.nytimes.com/2017/08/28/us/politics/trump -police-military-surplus-equipment.html

Hein, J. F. (2013). *Inside internal affairs: An in-depth look at the people, process & politics*. Flushing, NY: Looseleaf Law Publications, Inc., p. 205.

Korte, G. (2015). Obama bans some military equipment sales to police. *USA TODAY*. https://www.usatoday.com/story/news/politics/2015/05/18/obama -police-military-equipment-sales-new-jersey/27521793/

LeVine, M. (2001). 9/11: One year later. 10 Things to Know About Terrorism. *Alternet.org*. https://www.alternet.org/search/?q=LeVine%2C+M.+%282001%29 .+9%2F11%3A+one+year+later.++10+Things+to+Know+About+Terrorism.+

Liang, Q., & Wang X. (1999). *Unrestricted warfare: China's master plan to destroy America*. Beijing: PLA Literature and Arts Publishing House.

Regis University. School of Contemporary Liberal Studies. (2016, March 17). What causes someone to exhibit criminal behavior? Denver, CO: *Regis Criminology Programs*. https://primusaplang.wordpress.com/2017/09/27/what-causes-someone -to-exhibit-criminal-behavior-regis-criminology-programs-17-mar-2016-criminology -regis-educriminology-programsresourcescrim-articleswhat-causes-someone-to/

Ross, J. (2016). Two decades later, black and white Americans finally agree on O.J. Simpson's guilt. *The Washington Post*. https://www.washingtonpost.com/news /the-fix/wp/2015/09/25/black-and-white-americans-can-now-agree-o-j-was -guilty/?utm_term=.ad5deb90e64b

Surgeon General, Office of. National Center for Injury Prevention and Control. National Institute of Mental Health. Center for Mental Health Services. (2001). *Youth violence: A report of the Surgeon General*. Rockville, MD. https://www .ncbi.nlm.nih.gov/books/NBK44293/#A12607

White House, The, Office of the Press Secretary. (2015). *Executive order—federal support for local law enforcement equipment acquisition*. https://www.bja.gov/publications /LEEWG_Report_Final.pdf

Wright State University. (n.d.). *Code of Hammurabi. c.* 1700 B.C.E. Dayton, OH. http: //www.wright.edu/~christopher.oldstone-moore/Hamm.htm

WSMV-TV News. (2017, November 25). Police arrest accused serial bank robber after Saturday robbery. Nashville, TN: *News4 Nashville*. https://www.wsmv.com /news/police-arrest-accused-serial-bank-robber-after-saturday-robbery/article _574deb40-8a16-5c9b-a292-47b6ad4f2bf5.html

Wyllie, D. (2015). 3 crucial points about Obama's evisceration of the 1033 Program. PoliceOne.com https://www.policeone.com/patrol-issues/articles/8550404-3 -crucial-points-about-/

Chapter Six

SELF-UNDERSTANDING

Let me be clear: as I have said repeatedly, I do not believe all police officers are bad, nor do I believe most are bad. But there must be a transparent, impartial and fair system to judge those that engage in criminal or unethical acts.

Al Sharpton
Civil Rights Activist

Many in the white community might think Reverend Sharpton is a rabble-rouser, but most would likely agree with his statement. Since the inception of criminal justice systems centuries ago, much discussion has been held about police authority, their methods, culture and accountability. In modern times responsibilities seem to be misunderstood by citizens served and by the police themselves. A police officer is, first and foremost, a public servant. Duty to the community and public service should be on the mind of every officer. That might be difficult to comprehend for some as the headlines explode with stories of violence; foul, hateful, and deadly actions by citizens officers are sworn to protect. There are only a minority of officers, however, who face violence frequently. The vast majority of officers, even in the most populous cities, do not address crime as much as they do the social ills of society. Likewise, there are only a minority of citizens—a subculture who spew hate and violence.

Remember the officer Norm Stamper spoke to who said he would do whatever it takes to make it home at the end of the shift? I received a similar response when I told a police detective, a man I have known for decades that I was writing a book about police responses to Black Lives Matter criticism. I told him I thought S.W.A.T. and the militarization of law enforcement has contributed much to the agitation between police and people of color. He became defensive, raised his voice and became irritated and excited. "What do you want us to do, wear a tutu to confront violent criminals? I am not going to sing Kumbaya, My Lord with people who have guns and knives who want to kill me . . . it seems too many outsiders are trying to solve problems . . . so what if we have military type clothes, weapons and equipment . . . high schoolers can get them, I think more parent training is needed first." Although I must agree with his last statement, my friend, like many officers, does not understand the compromise that must be reached to stop violence and killing. Currently there is a vicious cycle where each side is afraid of the other. He is blind to the fact police officers are authority figures with many powers, the power to take away a person's freedom and the power to legally take a life. A police officer cannot be compared to a teenager wearing a costume. A police officer can be a role model for others to look up to, but many are not. My friend is programmed, like many others, to become defensive when American policing tactics are questioned (Hein, personal communication, 2018).

WHO IS TO BLAME?

American policing cannot be blamed for the disintegration of civility and lack of respect for the rule of law. It can be blamed, however, for spewing hate, disrespect, intimidation and deadly violence to parts of society that are not part of the criminal element. It should be obvious the way policing is conducted in the United States in many areas is not working. Occupying force policing considers everyone to be a suspect of some criminal activity, but this tactic only increases citizen apprehension.

The police are in the center of society, between the good and the bad, dealing with its objectionable, offensive evils. At its worst, officers oppose criminals who will do what they do—rob, rape, assault, murder—until they are stopped. At the other end of the spectrum are citizens and politicians who want law and order. Police are caught in the middle of this complex, dynamic interchange and seemingly criticized from all angles for some actions taken. Over time, law and order politicians have passed laws, awarded grants, created committees, councils, study groups and held forums to confront a seemingly unsolvable problem: unwanted or increasing crime. As we have already discussed, over the last five decades American policing has been given military equipment of all sorts, billions of dollars, increases in personnel and enjoyed a wide berth to keep the peace in society. After decades of encouragement to get tough on crime, it now seems police are not only faulted for poorly confronting crime, but how they address a violent society. American policing has done everything asked of them by the citizens and crime-fighting politicians who gave them the military equipment, the billions of dollars, the increase in personnel and the wide berth. Policing has always been faulted for bias; now the police are faulted for being too militaristic, valuing the seizure of assets over the constitutional rights of citizens and, of course, using frequent force for minor crimes and deadly force too often on the wrong suspects.

COMMUNITY POLICING IS PROACTIVE, NOT AGGRESSIVE

It was not supposed to be this way. During the violent times of the 1960s and 70s, crime fighting politicians introduced their focus to address increasing lawlessness, while others introduced community policing to enlist neighbors to help prevent and solve crimes. The increased militarization of policing is contrary to community policing where the strategy is to build ties to the community to work together and problem solve. As the U.S. Department of Justice, Office of Community Oriented Policing Service states:

> Community policing entails developing partnerships between law enforcement agencies and the communities they serve so they can work collaboratively to resolve problems and build community trust. It is a philosophy that promotes organizational strategies that support the systematic use of partnerships and problem solving techniques, in order to proactively address the immediate 5 conditions that give rise to public safety issues such as crime, social disorder, fear of crime, and satisfaction with police services. (U.S. Department of Justice, 2017)

The DOJ Office of Community Oriented Policing Services has organized community oriented policing into three parts:

- Partnerships between people and organizations to find solutions to problems and develop greater trust in police.
- Organizational metamorphosis to support the community-oriented strategy.
- ". . . proactive problem solving in a systematic and routine fashion. Rather than responding to crime only after it occurs, community policing encourages agencies to proactively develop solutions to the immediate underlying conditions contributing to public safety problems. Problem solving must be infused into all police operations and guide decision-making efforts. Agencies are encouraged to think innovatively about their responses and view making arrests as only one of a wide array of potential responses." (U.S. Department of Justice 2018)

Since there is no one definition of community policing, a conflict was realized when some departments began using S.W.A.T. as part of their community policing strategy, purportedly to keep the peace.

As constitutional rights are violated, police militarization continues, billions of dollars are spent on a failing drug war, and the crime rate and violence in many cities fluctuates between bad and worse. Many in American policing are not keeping the peace but enflaming civil disorder. Aggressive, militaristic policing with no regard to the sensitivities of citizens continues to cause citizen resentment directly related to these failures.

Any officer in the world knows, or should know, the best way to fight crime is to have sources of information, optimally prior to commission of a crime. People who know the neighborhood, who know the comings and goings of many who commit crimes. Sources with close ties to the neighborhood who are the life blood of policing and controlling crime. Agitating the very people a department serves does not help in recruiting informants useful in stopping or solving crime. Showing respect to others can and does solve crimes.

NOT EVERYONE HAS A CODE

For a law enforcement officer respect should be a deferential courtesy to others. It does not mean friendship although it could. For an officer respect might mean listening to a citizen before making a decision, not calling them derogatory names, shouting at or insulting them. It could also mean not being overly aggressive when aggression is not necessary. Many citizens have seen officers who shout while directing traffic, incite a situation rather than calm it, or become unpleasant when an order is not immediately and unquestionably obeyed. An officer must also understand that he or she not only is a public servant but has a code of ethics, while the public has no code and many times a far different culture than the officer's. Officers who were not raised in poverty but work in more impoverished areas can experience a culture nothing like the one in which they were raised. Considering the historical relationship some have with police, certain cultures might have a natural tendency to show contempt or a reluctance to comply with simple instructions.

Respect, however, can be different for different people. Respect should always be on the mind of any public servant, but for a police officer respect might last as long as the so-called New York second, the shortest possible measurement of time. As soon as it is determined respect is not appropriate, none is given. An officer must also understand what BLM or any protester is asking. Is indignation being expressed for those who rob, rape, assault or murder, or for those being shot who, seemingly, are no threat to police?

NO PLACE FOR JACKASS POLICING

Kendrick Lamar, also known as K-Dot, said when he was a teenager the majority of his interactions with police were not good. Some were good, but they were few and far between. He met some good officers, ones who were actively trying to protect the community. But others, like ones in and around Compton, California, who never met him before, they were not good at community-police relations. He was just a kid wearing nondescript clothing, but the police were tough and aggressive because he was only a teenager. K-Dot was the victim of occupying force policing also known as jackass policing.

Threats to officers are real, but many threats are self-created because of biased, aggressive policing, no or little maintenance or continuing education, or training that develops thoughts, with accompanying behavior, that everyone is a threat. Much has been said about de-escalation tactics to calm volatile situations, but some training seems to emphasize running towards the sound of the guns and fighting the battle rather than maintaining order, keeping the peace and enforcing laws. There must be some legitimacy to police, but in many isolated, detached areas, whether rural or in a large city, the police are considered outsiders, to be feared, to be avoided, disobeyed. The community is isolated from the police and some officers are content to fight the fight and continue the isolation.

In 2014, while an online adjunct university instructor of criminal justice I electronically interacted with a student who brought the following police actions into a classroom discussion. While responding to another student's positive experiences with a southern California police officer, this student who was not afraid to speak her mind and related a story, off topic, that disturbed me. The story troubled me because in the classroom I focused on how today's law enforcement officers serve the community. Lessons on the negative aspects of law enforcement such as misconduct, bias, abuse of authority and entitlement are minimal. However, in the classroom we did discuss attitude, perception and interpersonal communication. We also discussed the advantages of the community policing strategy where officers strive to know and have positive interactions with the people in the community. Over time I heard similar stories like the one told by this student, but in 12 years as an online instructor, a student never was as outspoken to describe what it is like to interact with local police officers. At the time the student lived in a middle class, diverse area with a slightly less Caucasian majority population. The student told me when she read another student's discussion on positive interactions with a police officer she was prompted to reveal her experiences and those close to her with police officers in her home town (Hein, personal communication 2014). The name of the department and the student will remain anonymous. The following is what the student related to the class:

> I am very familiar with the police here and (how) they unfortunately treat the public in an unprofessional manner. When a police officer is encountered here you cannot get a courteous hello. Not to mention they have nasty attitudes. I realize they have a tough job, but if you don't like your job, then don't do it. If you can't be courteous to the public then you shouldn't be in the field. When driving after 11 pm in your neighborhood, you can count on having a negative police encounter. Police here drive with no headlights on, going very slowly like creeping down residential streets just looking to mess

with anybody who may drive by or be walking by . . . they boom their huge bright spotlight right in your face so you are blinded. If you get pulled over you can count on really mean abrasive harassment. They intentionally try to intimidate the crap out of people. . . . If you ask a question you are told to shut up, not give me a moment, but shut up is what you get. You generally never get an answer to why you are being pulled over. If you refuse to tell them where you are coming from or where you are going, you get told to get out of the car and they put you in the back of their car. If you refuse to allow an officer to search your car, you are told to allow the search or you are going to jail. Officers instill fear into the public . . . they love (the) power play. I have never once had a pleasant encounter with officers here. (Anonymous, personal communication 2014)

The police mindset of conqueror rather than defender and guardian isolates an officer from the very people the officer should be embracing. What this student experienced in her neighborhood is jackass policing. The ends do not justify the means and only further separates citizens from police and increases already centuries' old distrust.

REGRESSIVE PULL

This turmoil adds to the revolving-door syndrome in the criminal justice system where some commit a crime, are convicted and, after serving a jail sentence, commit another crime and the events start again. This can also be said about the relationship some officers have with certain citizens. Some citizens, through interaction with aggressive and tyrannical police officers—officers who commit illegal acts while enforcing the law—have learned to despise police and disrespect their authority. This attitude can be expressed by petty or hardened criminals but also by law-abiding citizens. In a like manner, a police officer, through interaction with petty or hardened criminals, along with law-abiding citizens who despise police and disrespect their authority, have learned to suspect, distrust, criticize and fear them. Because of this frustration, some officers are drawn into a regressive pull.

As stated in *Inside Internal Affairs: An In-depth Look at the People, Process & Politics,* "The egregious and illegal behavior of police officers in many cases demonstrates a behavior called regressive pull. In a law enforcement sense, regressive pull [occurs] when an officer spends a great deal of time with the criminal element and begins to act like a criminal. More accurately said, an officer will disregard policy directives, common sense, and the law and commit criminal acts while enforcing the law" (Hein, 2013).

In 2016, a report, titled *Police Integrity Lost: A Study of Law Enforcement Officers Arrested,* was published detailing five types of crimes committed by sworn law enforcement officers during the years 2005 through 2011. The five types of crimes are: sex-related, alcohol-related, drug-related, violence-related and profit-motivated. Surprisingly, the study relied on Internet searches because there was no official data available for research purposes (Stinson et al., 2016). According to the report, the purpose of the project was to encourage police integrity by acquiring an increased understanding of crime by sworn officers and their department's response to arrest.

The study found three observations about police crime: a) police crime is not uncommon. From 2005-2011, the study identified 6,724 cases representing 5,545 sworn officers who were arrested. The arrested officers were employed by 2,529 state and local departments located in all 50 states and the District of Columbia. The officers were arrested at a rate of 0.72 per 1,000 officers and 1.7 per 100,000 of the population nationwide (Stinson et al., 2016); b) police crime is an occupational hazard, i.e., regressive pull is real. Police work can tend to lead some officers into various types of criminal behavior; and c) police crime is complicated and has many variables. The wide scope of police crime is confirmed by the intricate network of variables and predictors associated with conviction and job loss.

The data collected identified an unparalleled number of police crimes in a wide variety of jurisdictions and departments by hundreds of sworn police officers. The data also highlighted that police crime is "largely the product of opportunities" and is derived from the fact that officers work with little supervision and not much public visibility along with the experience of citizen interactions while exercising "considerable power and authority" (Stinson et al., 2016).

No effort to collect data can possibly determine the true number of police crimes. To better understand the data collected for the seven-year period from 2005-2011, one must consider the number of sworn officers and state and local departments in the United States. There are about 750,000 sworn officers in about 18,000 state and local departments. In seven years, 5,545 officers were reportedly arrested for police crimes. That is an average of 792.1 officers arrested in each of the reporting years. This figure represents slightly more than 0.1% of all sworn officers. Although one police crime is too many, near 0.1% per year of officers who commit police crimes is not statistically significant, but regressive pull is apparent. Saying not being significant may have raised eyebrows, but 0.1% of a profession which interacts with citizens who rob, rape, assault and murder means that 99.9% of sworn law enforcement officers were not arrested for a police crime, on average, during the reporting years (Stinson et al., 2016). However, the turmoil persists because of aggression and disrespect.

I MIGHT BE A BAD GUY, BUT YOU ARE RESPONSIBLE FOR MY SAFETY

Much of what surrounds the relationship between American policing and the black community is the need for both sides to show respect to the other. This might be another hard contention for some officers to understand, but respect after apprehending a hardened criminal is as important as showing respect during a traffic stop interacting with an otherwise honorable citizen. Freddie Gray in Baltimore may have had a history of arrests, but officers were obligated to respect his safety and place him in secure custody after arresting him. In 2015, Gray died from a spinal cord injury several days after being transported in a police van. A medical examiner deemed Gray's death a homicide because of officers' omission to follow newly enacted safety procedures to secure him during transport.

Six police officers were charged by the Baltimore state's attorney with various crimes including manslaughter and murder. All were cleared of the charges. A federal civil rights investigation was unable to prove the officers willfully violated Freddie Gray's rights. After Gray's death a sign was discovered in a police prisoner transport van that read: "Enjoy the ride, cuz [sic] we sure will!" We submit the sign is a sure indication of careless disrespect of arrestees whom officers are entrusted to protect.

We could not discuss the death of Freddie Gray without again discussing the sodomization of Abner Louima and the death of Laquan McDonald. As we mentioned before, Louima was beaten and sodomized with a broomstick in August 1997. New York Police Department officer Justin Volpe, with the help or at least knowledge of three other officers and a sergeant, shoved a broomstick into Louima's rectum and mouth, causing serious injury resulting in a 2-month hospital stay. During the attack we are sure Louima was screaming in pain, but no one interceded. Louima's injuries were ignored, most likely by numerous other officers and supervisors. Louima was not taken to a hospital until the next day.

Former Chicago police officer Jason Van Dyke shot Laquan McDonald 16 times while McDonald was carrying a knife. As previously mentioned, there is much controversy over the shooting because of a withheld video and the fact other officers attempted to cover up actual events. Reportedly, Van Dyke fired the shots as the suspect was lying on the ground facing away from the officer. Conversely, Volpe most likely did not make a snap decision to sodomize Louima. Our point is that from experience we know some officers believe they can get away with any type of abuse because supervisors ignored many previous acts of misconduct. From experience we know some supervisors avoid confronting questionable actions. From experience we know some supervisors like the stripes, or the silver or gold bar and the raise in salary, but they do not want the responsibility. Some supervisors are uneasy about supervising or afraid to do so. Some 'leaders' neither lead nor manage a difficult situation. They do not want to deal with challenging personnel issues. Bad behavior can escalate until a concerned supervisor or the criminal justice system demands an end to the conduct.

The fact that these acts of misconduct happened and other officers attempted to cover up the actions of Volpe and Van Dyke confirms there is regressive pull, a blue wall of silence, jackass policing and certainly poor training and distant supervision (Franklin & Hein, personal communication, 2019).

The death of George Floyd seems to be an extraordinary example of police improper use of force. It is notable for several reasons. 1) Much of the arrest of Floyd was video recorded. 2) Although Floyd may have committed a crime prior to his arrest, Floyd by all accounts was not a hardened criminal but a well-liked member of the community. Although he did not appear to be resisting arrest, he may have struggled with police when he was in the back seat of a police vehicle. It is unclear how he exited the vehicle, but iPhone video shows him being restrained on the ground by three of four officers on the scene. 3) Video clearly shows Floyd pleading for his life, the officer apparently most responsible for Floyd's death kneeling on Floyd's neck, reportedly for almost nine minutes. 4) As the officer looks at the camera, he seems to be unconcerned, almost empowered as he seemingly abuses and, in fact, may have been a factor in the death of Floyd. Since the officer is only accused of the death of Floyd, we reserve the judgment to the courts in the state of Minnesota. Certainly, the officers involved did not appear to be concerned with the safely of Floyd after he was taken into custody (Franklin & Hein, personal communication, 2020).

In any department there are good and bad officers. Some officers are exemplary, and the chief might wish the work performed by the officer could be imitated by all. This model officer cares about the perception of the police in general and makes every effort to conduct him or herself as professionally as possible, treats everyone fairly, and serves citizens with pride and respect. (As you read the last sentence, we hope you have not forgotten about the relationship between respect and the definition of the New York second.) Then there are the bad officers who do not serve citizens as they should, but instead show bias, disrespect and anger. Some go beyond misconduct and are intentionally dishonest and callous to those they supposedly serve. Citizens must understand the dilemma and the hard truth to which many officers are exposed: the reality of confronting intense hatred which some find difficult to deal with.

Some officers have a difficult time respecting others, and not much has changed over the centuries. History is replete with examples of police disrespect of citizens, whether it is a general indifference or the focused disdain of Rodney King. King and many others have offered the bait and many a cop has taken it. Television character Lt. Anita Van Buren on the NBC drama "Law & Order" once said, "A good cop never takes the bait and never escalates." Some officers just do not understand the bait, but they do react to it which keeps the cycle alive.

YOU KNOW IT BUT ARE NOT SUPPOSED TO SAY IT

The closed circuit in many communities continues and it is difficult to break. There is ongoing criticism of the police for abusive, sometimes deadly tactics. At the same time there is a culture in many communities where life has little value and where there seems to be no tomorrow. After a holiday weekend of violence, Chicago Police Superintendent Eddie Johnson said, "It's not a police issue, it is a society issue. . . . Impoverished neighborhoods, people without hope do these kinds of things," he said. "You show me a man that doesn't have hope, I'll show you one that's willing to pick up a gun and do anything with it. . . . Those are the issues that's driving this violence. CPD is doing its job. . ." (Gorner et al., 2016).

Most would agree with Superintendent Johnson, but most would also suspect that Johnson had his hand slapped and a finger in his face for saying what was on his mind. Seventy-one percent of Americans polled believe political correctness has done more to suppress needed discussions important to our society. On the other hand, 28 percent of respondents believe political correctness has decreased the chances of offending others (Ekins, 2017). There is no argument that there are many ills in society with no known or difficult fixes, but some in society would prefer to avoid a transgression rather than fix a centuries' old, dysfunctional subculture.

A jurist in Tennessee joined Superintendent Johnson in placing blame. Reported in the Clarksville, Tennessee *Leaf-Chronicle* on January 4, 2019, Judge Wayne Shelton stated, "Black men are more dangerous to other black men than white Klansman [Ku Klux Klan] ever were. . . ." He went on to say that "he's sick and disheartened by what he sees as a lack of respect for human life, especially among young black men willing to shoot at one another for little or no reason." Although he has been saying that "black lives matter" for years, he lamented that no one is listening (Ingersoll, 2019).

'Rules of right conduct' and 'a police officer must be held to a higher standard than others' are frequently used, trite but true statements. However, American policing is not perfect. Because of the work environment and the human factor of both citizen and officer, it will never be mistake-proof. Some unprofessional actions by police are deliberate, while some are just dumb mistakes. Some officers are outwardly biased, others might be unconsciously so. Some officers are poorly trained with inadequate leadership. Some are condescending and disrespectful. Some citizens are equally disrespectful and can take baffling actions in response to police commands. An indifferent response to a puzzling action can end with a dire conclusion.

An officer must understand the many cultures he or she faces in the 21st century. A contemporary officer must comprehend different values displayed by others and be concerned with a citizen's sense of honor and respect. Law enforcement, however, cannot right itself alone. There must be a like response of understanding and improvement from the black community.

OFFICER, YOU AND I ARE THE SAME, BUT YOU DON'T KNOW IT

As a deputy sheriff in the 1970s I had the occasion to interact with a young black man outside a bar. The man, along with dozens of others, was a witness to a fight that was soon concluded upon arrival of the police. The man approached me and said, "I am a man and you are a man." At the time I did not fully understand the statement. I merely said something like, "yes, I know" or "sure." I did not know there is a history to the declaration. According to the contemporary online news service OZY.com, the proclamation "I am a Man," took its place in history in February 1968, when protesters took to the streets during the memorable Memphis sanitation worker's strike. I say memorable because Dr. Martin Luther King, Jr. was in Memphis to lend support to a demonstration by sanitation workers to demand unionization. Dr. King was murdered the day after he gave his "I've Been to the Mountaintop" speech. Centuries before Memphis, in the late 18th century British abolitionists created a seal with the encryption, "Am I not a man and a brother?" The seal showed a black man kneeling most likely imploring someone to recognize his dignity. By the 1960s the statement became, "I am a man." With the advent of the gender-neutral BLM movement, the iteration became, "Black lives matter (Walsh, 2015). What I now understand is the man was asking me to show him respect (Hein, personal communication, 2018).

THE HOOD DISEASE

We agree with Al Sharpton that not all police officers are bad, and we are sure he will agree that not all in a black community are bad. There is, however, a dichotomy or vicious cycle between two cultures. One has a military mindset, is highly organized and is often overly aggressive and biased. This culture has authority, specific and increasingly improved training, policies, procedures and many rules of law to which to adhere. It often has poor supervision and a strong inclination to disregard proper actions. The corresponding culture can be united and well organized if formed into street gangs but is largely unstructured. This culture can also be overly aggressive and biased. Unlike the associate culture, it has no recognized authority and no code of ethics. Like the associate culture it has a strong inclination to disregard proper actions. At times, both cultures have a remarkable disrespect and lack of concern for the other. A number of members in either culture hold little value for life. Destructive interactions may cause members of either culture to experience physiological disturbances stimulated by pain, fear, sudden or prolonged violence. Historically, these disturbances have been called by many names: "shell shock," "soldier's heart," or "war neurosis" (Crocq et al., 2000). Since 1980, posttraumatic stress disorder has become a household name. History "tells us that a significant proportion of military casualties are psychological, and that witnessing death can leave chronic psychological symptoms" (Crocq et al., 2000).

More recently, posttraumatic stress disorder (or PTSD) has been recognized in first responders. The disorder can either be sudden or developed over time. The Mayo Clinic defines PTSD as "a mental health condition that's triggered by a terrifying event. . ." (Mayo Clinic, 2019). The American Psychiatric Association goes on to say "PTSD is a psychiatric disorder that can occur in people who have experienced or witnessed a traumatic event such as a natural disaster, a serious accident, a terrorist act, war/combat, rape or other violent personal assault" (American Psychiatric Association, 2018).

PTSD can also be diagnosed in residents living in many violent neighborhoods. Like first responders, citizens who have experienced acts of violence can have symptoms of PTSD: nightmares, obsessive thoughts; a constant sense of danger. "Kids with PTSD may compulsively repeat some part of the trauma while playing games or drawing, have trouble in their relationships with family members, and struggle in school" (Beckett, 2014). PTSD in citizens can be the same as symptoms in military members and first responders—they can experience an increased risk of aggression and violent behavior. Some who live in the inner city have their own name for PTSD: the "hood disease" (Cole, 2017). Although the cause and effect is unclear, researchers found that civilians with the disorder were more likely to be charged with a violent crime and jailed than others of similar backgrounds without PTSD. Researchers believe the neglect of PTSD in civilians is a public health concern and may be compromising public safety (Beckett, 2014).

Conversely, more and more avenues to help officers understand themselves are becoming available. An officer must learn to understand his or her emotions and response to stimuli. In some departments police families are also being helped to understand their family member's attitude and temperament, while help for citizens is stymied by limited mental health services. There is a continued isolation because of no compromise.

REFERENCES

Beckett, Lois. (2014, August 30). Black America's invisible crisis. ESSENSE/ ProPublica. https://www.essence.com/news/propublica-post-traumatic-stress -disorder/

Cole, N. L. (2019, February 3). Why inner city youth suffer PTSD: Structural inequalities of race and class produce poor health outcomes. *ThoughtCo.* https: //www.thoughtco.com/hood-disease-is-a-racist-myth-3026666

Crocq, M-A., & Crocq, L. (2000). *From shell shock to war neurosis to Posttraumatic Stress Disorder: A history of psychotraumatology.* U.S. National Library Medicine. National Institutes of Health. https://www.ncbi.nlm.nih.gov/pmc/articles/PMC3181586/

Ekins, E. (2017). The state of free speech and tolerance in America. Survey Report. Washington, DC: Cato Institute. https://www.cato.org/survey-reports/state-free -speech-tolerance-america

Gorner, J., Nickeas, P., Malagon, E., & Chachkevitch, A. (2016). Chicago top cop: It's society, not police. *Chicago Tribune.* https://www.policeone.com/Officer -Safety/articles/218799006-Chicago-top-cop-Its-/

Hein, J. F. (2013). *Inside internal affairs: An in-depth look at the people, process & politics.* Flushing, NY: Looseleaf Law Publications, Inc., p. 64.

Ingersoll, S. (2019). Judge goes on tirade about black-on-black crime, saying it puts klan to shame. *Clarksville Leaf-Chronicle.* https://www.theleafchronicle.com/story /news/local/clarksville/2019/01/04/tennessee-judge-tirade-black-crime-wayne -shelton/2482403002/

Mayo Clinic, Patient Care and Health Information. (2019). Post-traumatic stress disorder. Mayo Foundation for Medical Education and Research. https://www .mayoclinic.org/diseases-conditions/post-traumatic-stress-disorder/symptoms -causes/syc-20355967

Patients and Families. (2018). What is Posttraumatic Stress Disorder? *American Psychiatric Association.* https://www.psychiatry.org/patients-families/ptsd/what-is-ptsd

Stinson, P. M., Liederbach, J., Lab, S. P., & Brewer, S. L. (2016). *Police integrity lost: A study of law enforcement officers arrested. final technical report.* Institute of Justice, Office of Justice Programs, US Department of Justice, pp. 15, 21/22, 189/192. https://www.ncjrs.gov/pdffiles1/nij/grants/249850.pdf

U.S. Department of Justice. (2017). Office of Community Oriented Policing Services. FY 2018. *Congressional justification.* https://www.justice.gov/file/969011/download

U.S. Department of Justice. (2018). Office of Community Oriented Policing Services. *Problem solving.* https://cops.usdoj.gov/problemsolving

Walsh, M. (2015). *From 'I am a man' to "Black Lives Matter.' OZY.com.* http://www.ozy.com/flashback/from-i-am-a-man-to-black-lives-matter/61443

Chapter Seven

CHANGE CANNOT BE UNILATERAL

If we desire respect for the law, we must first make the law respectful.

Louis D. Brandeis
Associate Justice of the United States Supreme Court
1916–1939

There must be compromise to stop disrespect and killing. American policing sees the challenge and is making concessions, but with 2020 events, concessions are and never were enough. Since the killings of Ahmaud Arbery in Georgia and George Floyd in Minnesota and the protests that ensued, more than concessions are being made. Concessions by police are being overtaken by federal legislation and politically imposed mandates. While rampant corruption has diminished, misconduct because of poor training, mistakes with dire consequences and foolish actions because of apparent bias continues to bring uncertainty in police services. Changes are being made to supply better service, but modifications made to correct improper conduct cannot be unilateral.

ATTEMPTS AND MORE ATTEMPTS

Disputed police interactions with citizens and attempts to change police culture and improve training and tactics are centuries old. Many appointed groups were gathered, over time, to uncover corruption in local law enforcement to foster reform. First attempts to better policing were local efforts with the federal government only becoming involved when Bonnie and Clyde, Al Capone and others forced action. The Saint Valentine's Day Massacre in Chicago in February 1929 was the turning point of lawlessness in Chicago, and President Herbert Hoover was pressed into action by many business and political leaders who were exasperated by violent crime. We have previously mentioned the Wickersham Commission established by President Hoover to review the entire U.S. criminal justice system. The commission was empaneled not only because of increasing violence in Chicago but crime throughout the U.S.

Crime and corruption continued unabated and the Hofstadter Committee, conducted during 1931, was a New York State investigation of corruption focused on the New York City Police Department together with the Magistrates Court. In the mid-20th century, the Summerdale blue ribbon panel investigated the 1960 Summerdale Chicago Police district scandal where eight police officers operated a burglary ring with the Babbling Burglar, Richard Morrison. The panel subsequently recommended its chairman, O.W. Wilson, to become the Superintendent of Police. He modernized the department and served until his retirement in 1967.

The NYPD seems to have been a hotbed of corruption because yet another formal investigation was created. The Knapp Commission, formally known as the Commission to Investigate Alleged Police Corruption, was formed in 1970 by New York City Mayor John Lindsey. Two aspects became widely known from commission testimony, if not to the public, then to American policing. We have already mentioned Frank Serpico. He was the NYPD officer who uncovered corruption in the department, then through persistence caused the empaneling of the Knapp Commission. He is known as the first officer in the history of U.S. law enforcement to step up and give testimony about systemic corruption in policing. He became famous in 1973 when the book Serpico was published by author Peter Mass. His celebrity increased with the release of the movie *Serpico* in 1974. Meat-eaters and grass-eaters were two descriptions coined during testimony. As cited in the *New York Post,* the 1972 Knapp Report stated, "Meat-eaters are officers who 'aggressively misuse their police powers for personal gain,' while grass-eaters 'simply accept the payoffs that the happenstances of police work throw their way" (New York Post, 2015). In the mid-1990s another investigation of the New York City Police, this one called the Mollen Commission, formally known as the Commission to

Investigate Allegations of Police Corruption and the Anti-corruption Procedures of the Police Department, was established in 1994 by then Mayor David Dinkins. This was another attempt to address corruption in the New York City Police Department.

Not to leave out the U.S. West Coast, the Rampart Investigation, also known as the Rampart scandal, involved widespread corruption in the Community Resources Against Street Hoodlums (CRASH) unit in the Los Angeles Police Department Rampart Division in the late 1990s. Over 70 officers were involved in various acts of corruption.

CONSENT DECREES AND MORE TO REFORM

In more recent history consent decrees have been used by the U.S. Department of Justice (DOJ) to reform police departments seen by citizens as violating their constitutional rights. A decree is a court judgment agreed to by all parties involved in response to a lawsuit by DOJ. It is a contract where a police department, or other entity, admits the decree is a "just determination of their rights upon the real and proven facts of the case" (Rush, 2000). Because of controversial shootings of black men in recent years, consent decrees have been entered into with DOJ by police departments in Ferguson (2014), Cleveland (2015), Baltimore (2015), and Chicago (2015) among other cities.

Responding to a public outcry for criminal justice reform, then President Obama made changes to the criminal justice system to improve fairness while ensuring the safety of police and citizens. Through executive privilege his system changes included, but were not limited to, expanded education opportunities for the incarcerated, release of inmates sentenced to debatable overly long sentences and improved chances of employment and housing for people with criminal records (Martine, 2016).

In his January 2017, *Harvard Law Review* commentary it is not difficult to understand Barack Obama's passion for advancing criminal justice reform:

It's hard to deny the urgent need for reform, not just for policing, but for the entire criminal justice system. In 1980, there were less than half a million inmates in U.S. state and federal prisons and jails. Today, that figure stands at an estimated 2.2 million, more than any other country on earth. Many people who commit crimes deserve punishment, and many belong behind bars. But too many, especially nonviolent drug offenders, serve unnecessarily long sentences. With just 5% of the world's population, the United States incarcerates nearly 25% of the world's prisoners. We keep more people behind bars than the top thirty-five European countries combined, and our rate of incarceration dwarfs not only other Western allies but also countries like Russia and Iran. (Obama, 2017)

In 1986, after 16 years as a federal criminal investigator, I made the jump from investigating white collar crime, usually a non-violent activity, to investigating a more destructive offense, narcotics smuggling. Upon arrival in Miami, Florida I was assigned to the Florida Joint Task Group, an organization of Drug Enforcement Administration and U.S. Customs special agents. During my 2 1/2 year tenure I arrested or took part in the arrest of more than 50 people. Although some were high-level drug smugglers and dealers, most were pawns manipulated by others, sometimes unwittingly. All were charged with a federal crime for the possession with intent to distribute a controlled substance among other charges.

All who were found guilty were sentenced to a minimum of 5 years in federal prison. High-level traffickers may have received tougher sentences, but the pawns, the smugglers I arrested, all received a minimum 5-year sentence. Of all the people I arrested who I thought were pawns (and most of them were), I did not perceive one of them as a violent criminal. Most criminals that I arrested were from South and Central America eking out a living as best they could. All made more from one smuggling trip to Miami than they previously had earned in a year. I am not making excuses for anyone. They needed to be punished. However, for a non-violent criminal I believe 5 years was an excessive sentence. Multiply one excessive sentence by tens of thousands, then hundreds of thousands times the number of states that still have Three Strikes laws and you end up with over 2 million inmates in federal and state prisons, with many more in county and city jails. Many of the imprisoned are non-violent but still cost the numerous governments millions of dollars a year. One must also understand the additional costs of supporting families with a missing mentor and breadwinner (Hein, personal communication, 2020).

In recent years there has been an awakening that many non-violent people should not necessarily be imprisoned, and our burgeoning state and federal prison systems, along with their cost, are not sustainable. The 2017 budget for the U.S. Department of Justice was $29 billion, 30% of which, $8.7 billion, was spent on prisons and detention. The awakening was short lived since the presidential administrations changed hands.

THE COMPLEXITY AND POLITICS OF THE CRIMINAL JUSTICE SYSTEM

The Trump administration is dismantling some of what the Obama administration put in place, like a program for police departments to voluntarily ask for federal advice in improving a department to better serve citizens (Eder et al., 2017). This Collaborative Reform Initiative that not only helped to reform a department but improve police-community relations is being displaced by a get tough on crime approach that many would agree has not worked since inspired decades ago (Charles, 2017). In a free society, trying to beat someone into submission does not seem to work. Many would agree a military response with armored vehicles and assault rifles does little to quell riots, but it does encourage anger.

However, on December 21, 2018, President Trump signed the Criminal Justice Reform Act (Watson, 2018). With great bipartisan compromise as reported by CBS News, "The bill gives judges more discretion when sentencing some drug offenders and boosts prisoner rehabilitation efforts. It also reduces the life sentence for some drug offenders with three convictions, or 'three strikes,' to 25 years. Another provision would allow about 2,600 federal prisoners sentenced for crack cocaine offenses before August 2010 the opportunity to petition for a reduced penalty" (CBS News, 2018). If the suggestion is taken by the states, many would improve their fiscal foundation, but that will take more compromise.

A concession that would increase the professionalism of police would be to centralize or integrate police training. States have Police Officer Standards and Training (P.O.S.T.) certifications. They can be similar, but all are not the same. National officer certification is something we have not seen on any activist agenda. To standardize training, to require all officers everywhere in the United States, not just some officers in select departments, to receive certain training like we have described would certainly decrease some apprehension in the population. It would also stop 'gypsy cops,' officers who transfer from department to department just ahead of a disciplinary hearing for misconduct. But for concessions, for additional compromise, it seems someone would have to move a mountain.

WHO ARE THE POLICE?

The United States government is a union of states, which means governing is decentralized among the national, state and local governments. "This division and decentralization causes the system to be often unwieldy, slow moving, and redundant. . . . In 1997 the United States had 50 state, 3,043 county, 19,372 municipal, and 16,629 township governments" (USAonline, 2018).

Because of its history, the United States has an expanse of local control. Remember, in the United States there are approximately 750,000 officers in 18,000 law enforcement agencies. Every government agency and political subdivision can potentially have their own police department (Dees, 2014). The federal government has close to 100 departments, agencies, offices and services that have sworn officers who have arrest authority. There are a number of well-known organizations like the FBI, Secret Service and Homeland Security, but there are many more lesser known agencies like the United States Mint Police, the Smithsonian Police, the Postal Police and the U.S. Supreme Court Police. In the various states other than state, county, city and township police departments, there also can be water district police, transit police, school district police, along with state certified railroad [private] police departments (Dees, 2014). All this local control and varied police services causes a dilemma when discussing training, not to mention the hiring and selection process. Because each state has their own police standards, not all training is the same or includes essential 21st century training. Not all potentially valuable training is given because of bias, differences of opinion, demographics and funding. Because of local control, politics, and divisiveness some needed training is at best transitory, at worst neglected. But what is really causing this divisiveness that is readily seen in the media almost daily?

A VIOLENT SOCIETY, BIAS AND POLICE

According to the FBI there were more than 1.2 million violent crimes committed in the United States in 2016. This estimate is up 4.1% from 2015 (Federal Bureau of Investigation, 2016). It is a fact America is a violent society, or at least segments of it. It is also a fact Americans own more guns for personal use than citizens in any other country in the world. American police, arguably, have a tougher job than most other police in the world. Having more guns than other countries in western society causes a different dynamic in American policing. Police officers in the United States are taught, like officers anywhere in the world, to protect themselves and others. However, because of the proliferation of guns in the U.S. and the desire of many Americans, more than any other nationality, to own and publicly display, or at least conceal, a weapon in public, police are more on edge, more aware, more ready to act and, on occasion, overreact in a stressful situation. American police are taught anyone encountered has a high likelihood of having a gun. American police are also taught, through extensive training, to protect lives and property and control potentially dangerous situations. This extensive training is with weapons of all sorts along with learning many ways to use force to keep the peace and maintain order. As everyone knows this use of force, at times, is utilized in an unlawful manner.

The question many have asked is why would a highly trained police officer use force in a situation that clearly does not require force? American police are officially taught that everyone is a danger. Officers are also unofficially taught and have learned firsthand, on the job and through life, that out of all the people an officer may encounter blacks are the most dangerous. Many police officers are afraid of blacks. Many blacks are afraid of the police. Because of historical injustices and past personal encounters, many blacks are suspicious, wary and reluctant to have any association with police. Many, especially the young, are fearful of the police that seems to cause a callous disrespect.

We are going to say this again: some police officers are afraid of black men. An officer's fear of Philando Castile, a black man, got him killed. Castile was driving with his girlfriend and a taillight was out. He was pulled over and a Minnesota officer asked for proof of insurance and a driver's license. Castile handed the officer his insurance card and stated he was armed. The officer told him not to pull it out which he did not, but while Castile was searching for his license the officer shot him several times. This incident might be thought of as an anomaly, something out of the norm and not likely to happen again, but it seems the incident is not so unusual. In September 2016, a white, female Oklahoma officer shot and killed Terence Crutcher, an unarmed black man. The officer was charged with first-degree man-slaughter but was acquitted. The officer told reporters that she shot Crutcher because he was not following her orders and thought he was reaching for a weapon. She did not back away or seek cover but fired and killed Crutcher. There was no weapon. Then there is the Chicago officer who shot and killed Laquan MacDonald, a troubled black teenager, firing more than a dozen shots within seconds of arriving on the scene. The fear of people of color by police adds to the ongoing dilemma.

During my time in the Chicago Police Academy a probationary police officer (PPO) was killed while working with his field training officer (FTO). The two were dealing with the arrest of a suspected armed robber aboard a Chicago Transit Authority (CTA) bus. Prior to being patted down, the suspect shot the PPO in the back, killing him. Both the suspect and the FTO were armed with two handguns each, and a shootout ensued between the front and back doors of the CTA bus. The suspect was wounded and taken into custody. During a dis-cussion in my academy class it was revealed the PPO had an 'intense fear of colored people.' Since it was obvious the instructor who told us this was well aware of the PPO's fear, some of us had the brass to ask, 'Why did you allow him to pass and graduate from the academy?' We never received an answer (Franklin, personal communication, 2018).

How can an officer serve the public when that officer has a fear of people who he must serve?

WHAT GOES AROUND COMES AROUND

American policing and the black race are caught in a dilemma. This dilemma was created the first time enslaved blacks arrived in the American colonies in the early 16th century and is continuing today. What goes around comes around is an idiom. In this context it means when society treats blacks badly, eventually society will be treated badly in return. A like expression is 'as you sow, so shall you reap'. This can be said of white bigots and violent blacks who make life difficult for many blacks who have entered mainstream society or others who just want to live their life without controversy. Many people find this hard to understand and find it difficult to accept a compromise or discover a new reality.

Any Internet search for bias, or discrimination, or racism will reveal what some learned authorities, both black and white, say about the race issue. It is a daily issue for many. In fact, watching the media you have learned how racial slurs were thrown about at the University of Missouri in the fall of 2016, or how some white supremacists running for public office view the world or how force is used by police rather than diplomacy or de-escalation skills. In 2019, the General Motors Corporation offered a reward to anyone who could identify those who placed racist graffiti and a hanging noose in an Ohio auto plant.

American policing is not brutal and racist, but some officers can be brutal when not immediately obeyed. Some officers are deliberate racists; others are not but seem to be because of unconscious thoughts. Even when racism is not overt, a person of color must endure implied bias. We cannot say enough about implied bias because many people who believe they are racially impartial and broad-minded can be unknowingly biased by saying unintended comments or expressions that are at best belittling and at worst rude and insulting. Some readers of this book might believe the authors are guilty of bias because of our observations and descriptions, but we are biased against disrespect.

COLLATERAL DAMAGE

There is a right way and wrong way to enforce the law and maintain order. American policing must avoid damaging community and individual relations while performing their duties. There would be no argument that policing has, over centuries, used the wrong tactics to accomplish their mission. In the new era officers know every citizen interaction is an important public relations opportunity, but on occasion the advantage is not taken. Many officers overreact to situations that have been reported in the media. Many others use their 'game face,' his or her harsh attitude and air of authority for anyone, not just hardened criminals, which does a disservice to the community and to policing. It is obvious in many areas of the country, largely in the inner city, that law enforcement is not achieving success but merely making a valiant attempt to control periodic civil chaos. At times, officers who choose to use their game face for all citizens encountered end up harming community relations by failing to use their command presence judiciously. Officer insensitivity not only affects the target of the callous approach but affects everyone told of the interaction. Family and friends act accordingly when encountering police.

There is also a right way and wrong way to interact with a police officer, especially when the citizen is a person of color. We have discussed the 'talk," but some fail to heed the warning. Officer suspicions, fears and disrespect added to citizen suspicions, fears and disrespect causes collateral damage—hate for some and death for others. As we know, current stresses have caused many in American politics and policing to re-evaluate policies and have, notably, brought mindfulness to the forefront.

MINDFULNESS AND THE POLICE

Unquestionably, many police officers work under stressful conditions and some are traumatized by revolting, shocking or terrifying experiences. In response to recent incidents, American police officials are now looking for ways to reduce stress on the job. One new method is mindfulness and cognitive training. According to *Psychology Today:* "Mindfulness is the state of active, open attention on the present. When you're mindful, you carefully observe your thoughts and feelings without judging them good or bad. Instead of letting your life pass you by, mindfulness means living in the moment and awakening to your current experience, rather than dwelling on the past or anticipating the future" (Psychology Today, 2018).

As reported in the news website Quartz: "The technique's [mindfulness and cognitive training] goal [in training police officers] is to change the way officers manage stress and their emotions, emphasizing a deliberate, thoughtful response—and not a rash reaction. . . . Dr. Dan Siegel, clinical professor of psychiatry at the UCLA School of Medicine and founder of the Mindful Awareness Research Center at the university, told Quartz that there are three elements to mindfulness training: focused attention, open awareness—'the broadening of awareness so that there becomes a space between impulse and action'—and kind intention, or compassion" (Kozlowska, 2017).

According to the Mindful Badge website, mindfulness skills training fosters civility among police officers and department staff. Mindfulness training is a preventive measure that gives officers a greater capacity for self and situational awareness, perception, judgment and reasoning, along with a greater capacity for compassion, empathy and non-judgment. Reportedly, the training has reduced officer's stress, levels of anger, aggression and alcohol use. It has also improved sleep health and the ability to understand and share the feelings of others. Initial analysis of a study of 60 officers indicates levels of cortisol were reduced. According to *Psychology Today,* cortisol is a stress hormone and is public enemy number one. Elevated levels can interfere with learning and memory and increase weight gain, heart disease, cholesterol levels and blood pressure. "Chronic stress and elevated cortisol levels also increase risk for depression, mental illness, and lower life expectancy" (Bergland, 2013).

We have already mentioned the shooting of Michael Brown by Officer Darren Wilson in Ferguson. We know that the department was not the most ethical and preyed upon citizens rather than honestly protecting them. The city administration and department condoned constitutional abuses and used the court system as a cash cow. Confrontations between police and citizens and statistical goals given officers put enormous stress on everyone. The lack of humanity by officers also placed additional stress on anyone who passed through Ferguson and helped fuel a hatred between citizens and officers. Brown reportedly was disrespectful, and Officer Wilson was disrespectful in return. Or maybe the acrimony was started by Wilson, depending upon his initial approach to Brown, and apparently continued between the two. It is apparent the public perception is mixed depending upon who you want to believe. What ensued only flamed the fire of distrust. The Ferguson chief failed to make any statement of what occurred. No statement of any kind for weeks, while the media spoke to anyone they could find who could walk, talk and chew gun at the same time. There was a story and the media had to find something to report, so embellishments and lies became the headlines around the world.

A good part of why Ferguson fell apart after the shooting of Michael Brown is because the chief failed to make any statement to the public regarding what occurred. The chief's unwillingness to be timely and transparent allowed the press to develop their own story by uncovering 'eyewitnesses' who were still in bed when Officer Wilson shot Brown. The Ferguson media response could become a textbook example of what not to do as a police executive immediately after a high-stress situation.

A former chief I know responded to a shooting incident in a 21st century manner. An autistic youth attacked and wounded one of two officers who responded to a call for assistance from his parents. After the officer was slashed with a knife, the youth was shot and killed. The situation was a high-stress incident since the youth was black and both officers were white. Adding to the situational uncertainty, most city council members and the mayor were white. To lessen hints of racial bias, the then chief, who was black, told city officials to allow him to respond to all press inquiries. The chief's response was immediate and straightforward. Heated rhetoric soon subsided and race relations were unharmed (Franklin, personal communication, 2018).

Apparently, the Ferguson chief and mayor had little capacity for the seriousness of the situation and the stress it put not only on the department but on the citizens of Ferguson. They had plenty of time to address the shooting, but the lack of candor made a bad situation worse. Actually, a press conference was held, not by Ferguson officials, but by the chief of the St. Louis County Police Department. By the time Ferguson authorities relinquished their responsibility to another, efforts were already overcome by 21st century technology. The many social media outlets were already filled with rumors and 'alternative facts' which fit alternative agendas (Shults, 2014).

Certainly, the politically skilled and unskilled can take part in and benefit from mindfulness training to understand situational awareness and perception. Training can increase their capacity for thoughtful response to situations, compassion, empathy, non-judgmental thinking and their understanding of releasing stress experienced by an entire group or community because of citizen bitterness. Because of circumstances, American policing and many in the white community are realizing a change is needed, but a meaningful change cannot be accomplished in isolation.

REFERENCES

Bergland, C. (2013). Cortisol: why the "stress hormone" is public enemy no. 1. *Psychology Today.* https://www.psychologytoday.com/us/blog/the-athletesway /201301/cortisol-why-the-stress-hormone-is-public-enemy-no-1

CBS News. (2018). Senate passes bipartisan criminal justice bill. https://www.cbsnews.com/news/senate-passes-bipartisan-criminal-justice-bill-first -step-act-today-2018-12-18/

Charles, J. B. (2017). Justice Department ends era of pushing police reform. https://www.governing.com/topics/public-justice-safety/lc-sessions-justice -police-reforms-trump-doj-milwaukee.html

Dees, T. (2014). Why are there so many American local law enforcement characterizations and how do they all work together? *Quora.* https://www.quora.com /Why-are-there-so-many-American-local-law-enforcement-characterizations -and-how-do-they-all-work-together

Eder, S., Protess, B., & Dewan S. (2017, May 14). How Trump's hands-off approach to policing is frustrating some chiefs. *The New York Times.* https://www.nytimes.com/2017/11/21/us/trump-justice-department-police.html

Federal Bureau of Investigation. (2016). Uniform Crime Report. https://ucr.fbi.gov/crime-in-the-u.s/2016/crime-in-the-u.s.-2016/topic-pages/violent -crime

Kozlowska, H. (2017). U.S. police forces are practicing mindfulness to reduce officers' stress—and violence. *Quartz Media, LLC.* https://qz.com /1025231/police -departments-in-the-us-are-practicing-mindfulness-to-reduce-officers-stress-and- violence/

New York Post. (2015). 5 police corruption scandals that rocked New York City. ttps://nypost.com/dispatch/5-police-corruption-scandals-thatrocked-new-york -city/

Martine, G. E. (2016). Six ways president Obama reformed American Criminal Justice System. *NewsOne.* https://newsone.com/3590472/president-obama -criminal-justice-reform/

Obama, B. (2017). The president's role in advancing criminal justice reform: the urgent need for reform. *Harvard Law Review, 30*(3). https://harvardlawreview .org/2017/01/the-presidents-role-in-advancing-criminal-justice-reform/

Psychology Today. (2018). What is mindfulness? Sussex Publishers, Inc. https://www.psychologytoday.com/us/basics/mindfulness

Rush, G. E. (2000). "Consent decree." In *The dictionary of criminal justice* (5th ed.). Dushkin/McGraw-Hill.

Shults, J. F. (2014). How outdated police media strategy lost the Twitter-verse in Ferguson. *PoliceOne.com.* https://www.policeone.com/social-media-for-cops /articles/7479178-How-outdated-police-media-strategy-lost-the-Twitter-verse-in -Ferguson/

USAonline. (2018). State and local governments. http://www.theusaonline.com /government/state-local-government.htm

Watson, K. (2018). Trump signs criminal justice reform bill. *CBS News.* https://www.cbsnews.com/news/trump-signs-criminal-justice-reform-bill-live-updates/?ftag=CNM-00-10aac3a

Chapter Eight

ISN'T THERE ANY AGREEMENT?

. . . never lose sight of the need to reach out and talk to other people who don't share your view. Listen to them and see if you can find a way to compromise.

Colin Powell
Former United States Secretary of State

Students of history and anyone who likes Western cowboy movies know how Native Americans were discriminated against, moved from their land, lied to, starved and killed. There did not seem to be much effort, at least before the 20th century, to treat natives with respect, honesty and dignity. Even in the 21st century we are sure some would say Native Americans are still treated with contempt.

We told him about how our land had been stolen and our people were dying. When we finished, he shook our hands and said, "endeavor to persevere!" They stood us in a line: John Jumper, Chili McIntosh, Buffalo Hump, Jim Buckmark, and me—I am Lone Watie. They took our pictures. And the newspapers said, "Indians vow to endeavor to persevere." We thought about it for a long time, "Endeavor to persevere." And when we had thought about it long enough, we declared war on the Union."

Chief Dan George in the 1976 film,
The Outlaw Josey Wales

The above is a statement of frustration made by the film character Lone Watie explaining what eventually happened when the 'white man' failed to listen. We certainly do not advocate a war between law

111

and order and any culture, but as we said before, a conflict between authority and the overall black culture has been relatively constant since the first slaves arrived in North America in the early 16th century. We are discussing the relationship between a certain American black subculture, but resistance to authority is worldwide and multicultural for an abundance of reasons. Resistance can be caused by unfairness, injustice, unreasonableness, failures . . . everything we have already discussed. But for this discourse we will focus on how respect or the lack of it gives birth to and is the lifeblood of resistance to authority.

As we have seen, the federal government, businessmen, civic-minded citizens, religious clerics, politicians and intense social activists have all tried over the centuries to bring fairness and justice to the downtrodden and all people of color. Some have been earnest while others have been self-serving. Even earnest attempts cannot really be considered a success. The fact is, there seems to be no agreement on how to reach an understanding of differences in cultures and how to improve the socioeconomic status in which some people find themselves. In addition, there is a long-standing debate on the relationship between social class and crime. The debate focuses on whether lower socioeconomic classes account for more crime than others, or whether crime is spread among all classes. Some believe youths, with fewer opportunities than others, who are exposed to violence only tend to exhibit more violent behavior.

WHO OR WHAT IS TO BLAME?

President Lyndon B. Johnson, in his State of the Union Address given on January 8, 1964, stated: "This administration today, here and now, declares unconditional war on poverty in America. I urge this Congress and all Americans to join with me in that effort. . . . Our aim is not only to relieve the symptom of poverty, but to cure it and, above all, to prevent it. No single piece of legislation, however, is going to suffice" (Johnson 1964). President Johnson was ready to open the floodgates of government funding to solve the poverty problem. A little over a year later, however, then Assistant Secretary of Labor Daniel Patrick Moynihan authored a controversial report that some believed blamed the victim of poverty for their poverty. The report that became known as the Moynihan Report stated that "At the heart of the deterioration of the fabric of Negro society is the deterioration of the Negro family. . . . A fundamental insight of psychoanalytic theory, for example, is that a child learns a way of looking at life in his early years through which all later experience is viewed and which profoundly shapes his adult conduct. . . . The white family has achieved a high degree of stability and is maintaining that stability. By contrast, the family structure of lower-class Negroes is highly unstable, and in many urban centers is approaching complete breakdown" (Moynihan Report, 1965). President Johnson agreed with the report, but civil rights leaders took offense, saying that the problem was not a family structure issue but an issue of discrimination. The lasting conclusion: the report blamed the victim.

There seemingly was little agreement between old white guys running the federal government and black civil rights leaders, especially in the summer of 1965. The Moynihan Report was issued in March 1965 but was not made public for five months when the report was leaked to *Newsweek Magazine* in August. As chance would have it soon after the publication, as the Civil Rights Digital Library makes clear, the Los Angeles Watts riot began "which raged for six days and resulted in more than forty million dollars [sic] worth of property damage, [it] was both the largest and costliest urban rebellion of the Civil Rights era . . . the rioting claimed the lives of thirty-four people, resulted in more than one thousand reported injuries, and almost four thousand arrests before order was restored" (Civil Rights Digital Library, 2013). Soon after, President Johnson reconsidered his position and created programs to aid poor Americans, all Americans, which over the past 50 years likely have cost untold trillions of dollars. According to the Center on Budget and Policy Priorities the federal government, in fiscal year 2016 alone, spent $366 billion on so-called safety net programs. These are programs that assist the poor and working poor with food stamps, low income housing assistance and many other things.

Depending upon to whom you speak, liberals or conservatives, blacks or whites, rich or poor, the safety net programs have either helped the poor by assisting many to enter the middle class, or caused great harm for some by destroying the ambition to work and the family nucleus. Whatever your belief, federal aid programs have not relieved the symptom of poverty, cured it and, certainly, have not prevented it.

However, Dylan Matthews reported in *The Washington Post* that ". . . there was a huge fall in the poverty rate throughout the 1960s, and in particular after LBJ announced the War on Poverty in 1964 and followed up with Medicaid, Medicare, greater federal housing spending, and other programs to fight that war. In 1964, the [overall] poverty rate was 19 percent. Ten years later, it was 11.2 percent. . ." (Matthews, 2012). Over time, the [overall] poverty rate has ranged from 22.4% in 1959 when it was first estimated to 11.1% in 1973 (Center for Poverty Research, 2017). The poverty rate for blacks in 1959 was 55.1% and by 1969 it was 32.2% (Matthews, 2012). The latest [overall] poverty rate available, 2016, is 12.7% and 22% for blacks (U.S. Census Bureau, 2017). The economy, of course, has had a great effect on the poverty rate depending upon cyclical fluctuations.

It appears President Johnson's war to reduce poverty and its successions have had some success, but the last overall poverty rate of 12.7% and 22% for blacks seems to be a problem and apparently needs additional attention. Again, depending upon to whom you speak, if a focus is placed on the final 22% of blacks who are stuck in poverty, a reduction might take place that could cause a reduction of crime in poor black areas. Many would agree, both rich and poor, politicians and activists, this is a win-win situation. However, it seems there is a point of contention. Some would say poverty is caused by discrimination, the lack of investment by government and corporate America in poor black communities. Others would say poverty is caused by the disintegration of the black family.

RIGHT RULES OF CONDUCT

We all have heard stories of generations of families living in low-income housing or mothers having numerous children by various fathers, or students having discipline problems in school. Whether black or white, similar stories abound. Arguably, this is a dysfunction that is not part of mainstream society but does not necessarily cause crime. Other things that do not necessarily cause crime are low income, disregard for education, unemployment or a single-parent household. However, any police officer can confirm three aspects are re-occurring when addressing crime: mental illness which will not be addressed here, neglectful or uninvolved parents, and lack of appropriate mentorship.

Kendra Cherry believes "Uninvolved parenting, sometimes referred to as neglectful parenting, is a style characterized by a lack of responsiveness to a child's needs" (Cherry, 2018). These parents can be indifferent to a child's wants and requirements and offer little to no emotional support or supervision. They can be uninvolved with their child's activities, including school, because they may be too over-whelmed with their own problems (Cherry, 2018). Parental neglect can evolve into a crime because of acts or omissions that can endanger a child's health or life. Criminal neglect can include failure to provide food, clothing, medical care, education and general protection such as safeguarding a child from violent, abusive or predatory people (Law.com, 2020).

Appropriate mentorship is a close relative to involved parenting for youth to enter mainstream society as adults. A mentor is a trusted person, like a parent, teacher, friend, clergy or anyone who has a good, moral, beneficial influence on those mentored. Appropriate mentorship is advice on living a successful life and entering adulthood as an asset to society. Inappropriate mentorship is uninvolved, neglectful parenting. Inappropriate mentorship can also be given by people who lack known right rules of conduct. A criminal justice anecdote is the story of the burglar who enters prison to serve his sentence, associates with other criminals, and is released with a graduate degree in criminal behavior.

RULES OF CONDUCT ARE MULTICULTURAL

Disorder, crime, poverty and any other social ill or asset are parts of our overall society, not just part of one subculture; society is multicultural. More simply, the disintegration of the family is multicultural. In addition, rules of right conduct are not only multicultural but accepted internationally. Globally, it is understood the crimes of murder, theft and assault are wrong. But in some cultures, certain conduct is accepted. Many have heard after a business deal has gone wrong: 'Sorry, but business is business.' The one treated unfairly understands that the buyer must be wary and should act accordingly. Laws were enacted to bring order to the business world, but most entrepreneurs know their reputation is an intangible asset worth a great deal. A successful businessperson understands and follows widely accepted rules of conduct. An accomplished businessperson has a mental and emotional strength, a determination to succeed. They have the self-confidence and resolve to endure hardships, failures, and bad luck to continue to grow their business. American businesspeople belong to a subculture of American society but are part of the mainstream. Other subcultures of society, whether black or white, may not have the same determination or endurance and some are not members of the mainstream for various reasons.

THE MAINSTREAM

Mainstream society is a wide culture with common thoughts and accepted behavior. Members of the mainstream generally have similar values and ideas, in spite of the fact many belong to opposing political parties. Mainstream society believes in the rules of right conduct that includes aspects of the U.S. Constitution. The mainstream has gone through periods of extreme apprehension and anxiety because of the election of the current and immediate past president of the United States. The mainstream understands the rules of right conduct. The fact that *transparent* political maneuvering was according to the right rules of law implies the mainstream have similar morals and beliefs.

Many subcultures are part of the mainstream and many are not members because of poverty, the lack of education, a criminal conviction denying the right to vote, underrepresentation in the political arena, various illnesses and many other factors like values, ideas, morals and beliefs. As previously discussed, numerous government assistance programs have played a large part in bringing many subcultures into the mainstream. But there are some in any subculture who lack the determination, the stamina, the resolve, or mentorship to help themselves. There are still others who, for various reasons, do not want to be part of the mainstream.

THE PLUMBER'S BUTT EFFECT

Some believe the plight of many is because of unfairness, injustice or general discrimination. Others might say the disparity is caused by the fear some have of black equality. Still others believe the plight of some blacks is because of their choices and irresponsible actions. Whatever the reason, some members of subcultures, whether black or white, have an inordinate time freeing themselves from hardships. A subset of the poor black culture seems to be the most hardened. In an infamous speech, well-known comedian Bill Cosby, a person once loved by all, both black and white, stated things many in mainstream society were thinking about poor blacks. Cosby denounced their attitudes and behavior. He chastised them for not grasping and furthering civil rights successes. He berated them for dropping out of school, for wearing baggie pants that show their underwear and sometimes more like a plumber's butt crack, for fathering children out of wedlock and not parenting them, for valuing luxury items over items of necessity and for showing pride in their African heritage by giving their children names that are unrecognizable and hard to pronounce by mainstream society. He also assailed poor blacks for taking actions that embarrass their families, like stealing a piece of pound cake. His example labeled his remarks as the "Pound Cake Speech." He used the illustration of a youth being shot in the back of the head for stealing a piece of pound cake and embarrassing his mother (Sewer, 2015). Cosby's speech became infamous because he chided a group of people as a whole.

Neither scientific hypothesis nor methods offer suggestions or conclusions that cause people to believe or know that all poor blacks are as Cosby describes. The same can be said of Cosby's assertions that some poor blacks are as he depicts that may cause them to be estranged from the mainstream. To the contrary, poor blacks are not the victims of poverty or bad behavior or parenting but of discrimination. Just ask those who say so.

ARE YOU NOT BLACK ENOUGH?

Many of Cosby's assertions are not universal, but some of what he describes are generally recognized qualities of a subset of people, regardless of race, who display irresponsibility, a likely lack of education, shortsightedness, shortcomings in moral or ethical character, and plain thoughtless, foolish behavior. Since what some call his 'rant,' Cosby has been soundly vilified for not using his celebrity status to further civil rights achievements and condemn discrimination. At the time, Mr. Cosby apparently did not understand his reception would be underappreciated because he just is not black enough. To define not being black enough is difficult because not all people are alike. It includes more than actions, clothes and other material things. It also includes a philosophy, an attitude, a belief and a way of thinking. Not being black enough would be one who does not always side with blacks but might at times side with non-blacks or not agree with what other blacks might think. It seems not being black enough is being an independent thinker. One who is identified as not being black enough might be a black person who is part of the middle or upper class of the mainstream of America and is comfortable with their status. Any black person could be labeled as not being black enough, even some-one in the lower economic level of society, if the person is not shy of being critical of one who is black and finds fault in certain aspects of black culture. There is a struggle between what is right and good for the black individual contrasted to what might benefit blacks collec-tively. However, many mainstream blacks shy away from any contro-versy regarding race because they do not want to be insulted by oth-ers who use overbearing methods (such as social media) to intimidate and bully them.

Not only was Bill Cosby, a highly educated and wealthy black man, roundly criticized, but others have been criticized for not being black enough. Anthony A. Williams, the mayor of Washington, D.C. from 1999 to 2007, is another highly educated black man who also was discredited by some in the black community. Williams was an energetic leader who restored the city to financial stability and, in doing so, disaffected lower-income blacks. City home values rose, houses in deteriorating neighborhoods were renovated, and a bloated city budget was reduced eliminating some redundant positions on the payroll that displaced some black low-income families. In some respect, not being black enough sometimes means you are too edu-cated, too resourceful, or too "mainstream."

It is difficult for the black community to resist the 'circle the wag-ons' mode no matter who is the aggressor. Often the greater white society has put much effort into tearing down black leadership. During the civil rights struggle led by Dr. Martin Luther King, Jr., then FBI Director J. Edgar Hoover took delight in the fact he possessed incriminating and titillating audio recordings of some of MLK's more intimate moments with numerous women, none of whom was his wife. Some of this salacious information was actually sent to Dr. King's wife, Coretta, to exploit every opportunity to discredit him. For MLK to be successful in his quest for dignified treatment of people of color, there had to be a massive amount of circling of the wagons (Franklin, personal communication, 2018).

Sometime in the mid-1980s, I had occasion to discuss the newly created federal holiday honoring Dr. King with two white Chicago police sergeants. They both proclaimed that 'King was a tool of the Commies' and most 'colored' people did not support civil rights efforts. I now understand their opinions were strongly influenced by the efforts of FBI Director Hoover (Franklin, personal communication, 2018).

The black community was united in their defense of Dr. Martin Luther King, Jr. As the opportunities Dr. King strove for became a reality, the black community became more educated, knowledgeable and autonomous than in the past. Now that the community is more informed it must do a better job of supporting those who seek a better life for people of color rather than those, like a few sports figures and entertainers, who are destructive to black society as a whole. Normalizing vulgar, sometimes criminal behavior only hurts black children (Franklin, personal communication, 2018).

COSBY LED TWO LIVES UNTIL . . .

For decades Bill Cosby was a well-liked, revered comedian, actor and author. Apparently, also for decades, possibly for 35 to 40 years, Cosby was drugging, sexually assaulting and raping unsuspecting women. In April 2018, his confirmed guilt of aggravated sexual assault made him a convicted felon. Reportedly, Cosby's first criminal sexual action occurred in the mid-1960s and continued into the 21st century, possibly ending in 2008. The authors are not defending Cosby's actions. His actions are reprehensible, but there seems to be a connection between his Pound Cake Speech in May 2004 and accusations of sexual assault coming forth soon after. After being criticized for his thoughts, he continued, in 2004, his unapologetic oratory of what some would call his mentoring compassion, others would say betrayal to his people. Within months, in January 2005, Andrea Constand accused Cosby in a criminal complaint of sexual assault that eventually was dropped but was replaced with a civil suit. Beginning in February 2005, other women came forward, but nothing of criminal consequence happened. Then in 2014, black comedian Hannibal Buress created a routine that berated Cosby for finding fault in certain segments of black culture. Reportedly, after presenting the routine for a time with little attention, he recorded the show and encouraged his audience to view it again online. Soon after, in late 2014, another flood of accusers became public. Were public comments a public service or a way to discredit Cosby for being disloyal and not black enough?

What Mr. Cosby did not understand and what others do not understand is that it is difficult to criticize blacks, especially poor blacks. Poor blacks are widely considered the most discriminated against segment in American society. They are also seen as the most victimized by discrimination in America; at least that is the politically correct response to what many believe are the facts. Cosby also did not understand the culture of some blacks, especially young blacks, who do not dress like him or hold the same values. Cosby was speaking in the early 21st century, but his thoughts were still in the 1960s. However, black comedian Franklyn Ajaye said he hopes the black community understands Cosby's words as a call for blacks to take education more seriously, to conduct themselves with dignity and to show self-respect if they want to be more successful in racially hostile America. Ajaye believes Cosby made the statements out of tough love; that the messenger was flawed but not the message.

There is another message many law enforcement leaders have learned after the fact when offering an olive branch to the black community: just as blacks cannot be blamed for their fate, American policing cannot be criticized for inappropriate actions. Those who would try to narrow the divide between policing and the black community learn two things quickly: 1) exceptionally vocal, self-appointed representatives of black youth assert that young, poor, black criminals make poor choices because society has done them wrong and police, not young blacks, are to blame for whatever caused a black youth to be shot by an officer; 2) exceptionally vocal representatives of law enforcement rank and file maintain that American policing is not to blame for sometimes errant actions because they must confront young, poor, violent black criminals who make poor choices. Police leaders have stepped between the two factions in an effort to get someone, anyone, to listen in the hope things will change. You will find things are changing, at least in American policing, although not fast enough, but maybe not so much in the black community.

LET'S NOT SET THE STANDARD TOO HIGH

Michael Eric Dyson in his book, *Is Bill Cosby Right? Or Has the Black Middle Class Lost its Mind?* says Cosby places an overemphasis on personal responsibility (Dyson, 2005). That is a hard pill to swallow. Most people, unless you are talking about the ultra-rich, achieve success when they take personal responsibility for their actions. In fact, the Brookings Institution indicates that "Personal responsibility is the willingness to both accept the importance of standards that society establishes for individual behavior and to make strenuous personal efforts to live by those standards. But personal responsibility also means that when individuals fail to meet expected standards, they do not look around for some factor outside themselves to blame. The demise of personal responsibility occurs when individuals blame their family, their peers, their economic circumstances, or their society for their own failure to meet standards" (Haskins, 2009). Dyson goes on to say that in the abstract being hard working and responsible sounds fine, but swings in the economy sway against the poor. Poor performance in school or high dropout rates are caused by a segregated educational system and an inordinate number of black men in jail is because they are targeted for incarceration (Dyson, 2005). So, who is right? Maybe everyone is, but neither side is listening to the opposing position and there is little consensus to move forward, but there might be a sliver of hope on the horizon. There is a dispute brewing at the height of black consciousness.

IT'S OPRAH'S TURN ON DEFENSE

It seems Oprah Winfrey has had a running dispute with prominent blacks in the entertainment field. Certain entertainers promoting a type of music and the lifestyle the music stimulates have garnered her displeasure. Their style is not supported by her and was not seen on her television show. Oprah is a role model to many, mostly women, black and white. She is also considered a trusted voice of moral authority, a voice based on principles and truth. However, as did Bill Cosby, Oprah may have taken one step too far out of the protective circle of wagons.

When Oprah Winfrey still had her show on the ABC network, I applauded her for steadfastly refusing to book any gangsta rappers on the program. I have no doubt that Oprah, as I do, regard gangsta rappers as purveyors for the glorification of crime of all sorts, the contempt of law enforcement, profanity, sexual promiscuity, racism and the abuse of women. Many in the entertainment field, whether rappers or athletes, prey on the black community (and some in white society too) by glorifying disrespect. Many well-paid and highly praised black athletes and entertainers tell young people to 'be yourself and don't compromise.' They say this knowing that in the business world anyone is judged far more harshly than in the entertainment world. This can be especially true when a business is looking to diversify their workforce. What is acceptable in the entertainment or sports world would not get anyone past the application stage, especially if the applicant is from the black community. In some areas of the country, legislative efforts are being made to outlaw natural-hair discrimination in an attempt to protect black employees. The fact is, long braids and large uncombed afros are very likely to move many to the back of the employment line for some well-paid positions with high visibility, particularly in the business world. Employers are adapt at rejecting an applicant, particularly a black one, for a variety of reasons without revealing the truth (Franklin, personal communication, 2020).

In 2019, Oprah partnered with filmmakers and media outlets to produce a film documenting accusations that Russell Simmons, a black man and record executive among other things, sexually assaulted women. Soon after the film was publicly announced, Simmons and his supporters began a campaign to persuade Winfrey to distance herself from the project. A Simmons' supporter accused Winfrey of "only going after her own," asserting that by backing those who accused Simmons of wrongdoing she was abandoning the black community. Never mind the three women accusing Simmons of sexual assault were black women. Oprah eventually did drop her involvement in the film but reportedly not because of pressure from Simmons, but because of the credibility of a main witness (Sisario & Sperling, 2020).

Although Winfrey said she was not pressured to back out of the project but did what she believed was right, female accusers and others felt betrayed and believed "the most powerful black woman in the world is being intimidated." A representative for Simmons stated if defending against alleged wrongdoing is intimidation, then there is no justice (Sisario & Sperling, 2020).

The dispute has caused black women to question their place in the #MeToo movement and believe they are second best to black men who are brought into the criminal justice system. As one of the accusers of Simmons stated, "There is no one to protect us. There is no one to help us. And our own community turns against us when you dare to speak out" (Sisario, & Sperling, 2020). Simmons' accusers believe they were forsaken while Oprah believes she did, after careful consideration, the right thing. But doing the right thing does not end the story.

IS THE DESIRE TO CIRCLE THE WAGONS BREAKING?

Gayle King, reportedly Oprah Winfrey's best friend and an admired CBS journalist, also stepped out of the protective circle of wagons during an interview with Lisa Leslie, a WNBA player. Leslie was a close friend of Kobe Bryant, a Los Angeles Lakers' player who died in a helicopter crash along with his daughter and others on January 26, 2020. During the interview King asked Leslie about a previously settled sexual assault charge against Bryant (Bauder, 2020).

Kobe Bryant was an exceptionally talented basketball player who was loved by many. His death became a national tragedy. Numerous well-known black talents denounced King for asking whether Bryant's legacy was problematic because of an accusation he raped a woman in 2003. When responding to the allegation Bryant said he had consensual sex with the woman, apologized for his conduct and settled a civil lawsuit (Bauder, 2020).

However, he was a black man now being publicly criticized for alleged sexual misconduct. It seems King stepped over the line, but almost 16 years after Bill Cosby was berated for singling out and criticizing a black subculture, King was offered a hand of support. As the denouncements became warnings, even threats, CBS management stepped up to the plate and took a swing. Susan Zurinsky, president of CBS News, was not defending a scorned woman. She was not even defending a person who happens to be a black woman. Zurinsky was defending a journalist and every journalist's claim to the right of expression and freedom to inform the public (Bauder, 2020).

Gayle King is a journalist who reports the news, who educates the public and who may also entertain just because of her personality. She belongs to a highly regarded fellowship which most members take in a genuinely serious way. King is part of a profession which may be highly regarded because of individual notoriety and showmanship, but also because of the seriousness and the analysis of the subject matter. King was vilified by a number of celebrities, and received death threats, but was protected most likely because she is a journalist. Being a journalist may have put a crack into the precedent of outspoken blacks damning others for criticizing anything in the black culture.

On the other hand, Cosby created a firestorm when he shared his negative views of a certain black subculture. As a doctor of education, he expressed a thought many agreed with but apparently was too radical at the time. There was no movement to help the subculture Cosby identified, just one to defend it because the subculture happened to be black. Although Bill Cosby was known as a professional, but a professional in a theatrical way, he was not protected. Pundits went on the offensive and Cosby had no one to defend him; his profession did not afford him anything to hide behind. Circling the wagons stayed fast and Cosby suffered for it.

King did not express an opinion but submitted a probing, unquestioningly true inquiry about one person because it was her job. Gayle King, the journalist, took a shot across the bow, but her profession had to protect her. Her profession had to protect the public good or, maybe, just the right to ask the question. Hopefully, protecting the right to ask may have caused a crack in the circle of wagons because people are tired of others taking nasty shots for an opinion, or observation or a simple question.

It did not hurt, in at least in Gayle King's case, that Oprah Winfrey, the recognized media queen and King's close friend, may have interceded. However, we wonder how Winfrey and her reportedly closest friend could be embroiled in a spat with black entertainers at about the same time. The timeline is unclear, but the facts are clear and the reason suspect. Within weeks of Oprah distancing herself from a controversial documentary criticizing a black man, Gayle King seemingly criticized another black man and suffered for it. The suspect part is the fact two black women were involved in criticisms of black men, both accused of alleged sexual assault, and the same genre of black celebrity offered an aggressive offense to both. We believe a struggle is surfacing between black women and those in the entertainment industry who practice excess, especially in alleged misogyny and the degradation of women. Whatever the reason, we hope a break in the taboo for blacks to recognize or reveal fault in other blacks may have an end in sight. This end may open up a discussion to help people who seemingly cannot help themselves. There is another consideration, however, that is part of this debate.

YOU'RE NOT BLACK ENOUGH BECAUSE YOU'RE PART OF THE MAINSTREAM

United States military forces have a code of conduct. It is a code of ethical standards every military member is expected to adhere to whether in combat or in captivity. The written code includes six articles which detail doctrines which help keep our country safe and address how members of its armed forces should act in difficult situations. The code is not a regulation or law, but a guide for all members of the military, whether black, white, yellow, brown or red. If an individual can comply with the military code of conduct and other standards, the individual is welcomed. We have already discussed the standards anyone wishing to be part of mainstream society must follow. There is no written code for mainstream society, but society members expect others to adhere to certain standards. Mainstream standards are, as are military ethical standards, for all races. Being mainstream is not black or white but being part of a majority group that accepts the same prevalent opinions and rules of right conduct. If the individual can meet mainstream standards, the individual is welcome, but there is a downside if you are black. If the individuals are black, it is to their peril if their black roots are not firmly planted. The exception is not a mandate of the mainstream but of certain individuals in the black community who apparently feel threatened. According to self-appointed black authority, blacks who are part of mainstream society must adhere to a code that protects other blacks no matter what the transgression. Remember you are black. Thou shall not criticize.

Unendorsed black pundits have collectively determined blacks will not be criticized for any breach of right conduct by other blacks.

Bill Cosby offered what he thought was constructive criticism and he suffered for it. It does not matter he attempted, in his way, to help a certain subculture of black society. Oprah Winfrey was ready to take the step outside the circle but thought better of it. Gayle King completed the step but was saved by journalistic principle.

There is an abundance of people in the black community who are part of the middle and upper echelons of society. Many are proud of the fact they belong to mainstream society. Others who might seem to be in the mainstream are not because they declined the invitation. Some of the most prominent blacks who are not assimilating are in sports or the music industry; others might be in academia or professional writers. All are celebrities in their own way who apparently relish success but seemingly disdain sharing their success with what they consider to be a white society.

We understand some blacks still feel marginalized, and frequent media reports confirm why. Some in the black community want their 'own' music, art, their own awards; they want to protect their own culture and society should understand why. However, to protect parts of that culture that we have identified as a harmful subculture which embraces practices that are both physically and mentally destructive only enhances the marginalization of the entire black community. It seems as society strives to lessen the slope of inequity, some seek the status.

LIKE-MINDED, BUT NOTHING CHANGES

There seems to be an ongoing conflict in the black community, and Vice Admiral Jerome Adams, the United States Surgeon General, is the most recent scapegoat. In April 2020, during one of President Trump's televised coronavirus task force briefings, Surgeon General Adams gave advice to the black community, but, according to a vocal pundit, it was not retrospect, considerate, compassionate or thoughtful enough. Adams, when asked about the high percentage of blacks contracting the coronavirus in comparison to other racial groups, answered that "African-Americans and Latinos should avoid alcohol, drugs, and tobacco." In response, Linda Goler Blount, president and CEO of the Black Women's Health Imperative, questioned why Adams was not addressing and was personally outraged that "some 40 percent or more people . . . have underlying preventable chronic diseases?" (Bunn, 2020). Adams' remarks and Blount's retort came as health experts continue to focus on the inordinate number of African Americans who are dying from coronavirus.

Doctor Henry Louis Taylor, Jr., a professor and researcher at the University of Buffalo, stated, "It is irresponsible to talk about the elimination of drugs and alcohol without talking about eliminating the neighborhood-based social determinants that produce drug and alcohol abuse. . . . Adams statement is, at best, irresponsible and, at worst, reflective of systemic structural racism. . ." (Bunn, 2020). Doctor Pierre N. D. Vigilance, Associate Dean of Public Health Practice and Associate Professor at The George Washington University, was not elated "with Adams' comments but he attributed the backlash to Adams' association with the Trump administration" (Bunn, 2020).

I agree the surgeon general is backing the wrong horse. Because Adams is identified with the Trump administration, nothing he says will resonate well with most of the black community. Trump is the poster boy representing how many blacks see white people as a race. He often speaks first, with no idea how his words offend those persons he knows little about or has taken few steps to understand. Trump appears ignorant about people who are different from him. He has typically shown disdain for women, Hispanics, Muslims and other minorities, and let's not forget his referrals to continents and countries of color as 'shitholes.' President Trump has become the standard bearer and the face of a decidedly 'divided America,' but has said he has done more than any other president for the black community. Black unemployment was at a record low in May 2018, but according to AP Fact Check President Trump has exaggerated his role in black gains. Many economists consider the continued economic growth since 2009 as the primary explanation for hiring. The growth started during the Obama administration (Yen, 2019). The growth continued until the outbreak of the coronavirus pandemic. Neither the economic growth, nor the pandemic is Trump's making (Franklin, personal communication, 2020).

It is obvious Adams is far removed from 'the hood'—areas where grocery chains simply will not invest in the community. These same neighborhoods are where the big-box stores are closing. I suspect he is detached from parts of society like others are as members of the mainstream. In his defense, Adams has been focused on the overall effect of the coronavirus on the nation and was apparently not prepared for a question of such specificity regarding the black community. Then there is the fact that members of the Trump administration must measure their words carefully or risk the loss of their position along with vilification (Franklin, personal communication, 2020).

I suspect the surgeon general falls under the 'Bill Cosby syndrome.' It wasn't his message so much as how it was expressed. He did not discuss how social environment and a poor lifestyle contribute to a weakened immune system-an immune system which is susceptible to the coronavirus. He did not mention how the black community in Chicago makes up 30% of the population, but more than 50% of coronavirus cases and close to 70% of the associated coronavirus deaths are in the black community (Franklin, personal communication, 2020).

What I do not understand is why the black pundits attacked the surgeon general rather than approach him in private. It seems a united front would be better than an attack. According to the U.S. Department of Health and Human Services website, "The U.S. Surgeon General is the Nation's Doctor, providing Americans with the best scientific information available on how to improve their health and reduce the risk of illness and injury." When it comes to the black disadvantaged, it seems the most educated or the most talented would rather fight among themselves rather than help to solve the problem of poverty and all its ill effects (Franklin, personal communication, 2020).

JAMES COMEY WAS LEADING US
IN THE RIGHT DIRECTION

James Comey, the embroiled former director of the FBI, says American policing and the black community have long been separate parallel lines—the lines being closer in some communities and farther apart in others. He continues by saying the lines are arching away from each other every time a police officer kills a civilian. Comey has brought forth four 'hard truths' that he believes everyone should know. First, American policing should acknowledge it has been the enforcers of the status quo that abused the black community because people served and protected cannot forget the hateful, reprehensible history of oppression. Second, law enforcement needs to acknowledge everyone carries implicit bias—an unconscious bias that can lead to injustice. Third, he talks about regressive pull that can warp perspectives and lead to cynicism. (Remember, regressive pull can be demonstrated in an officer who spends a great deal of time with the criminal element and begins to act like a criminal.) Finally, "we all must acknowledge that the police are not the root cause of the most challenging problems in our country's worst neighborhoods, but that the actual causes and solutions are so hard that it is easier to talk only about the police" (Comey, 2018).

AMERICAN POLICING CANNOT DO IT ALONE

We hope the title of this section has raised some eyebrows. When was the last time you heard anyone in American policing publicly criticize the Black Lives Matter movement? It appears everyone in law enforcement, or at least the ones who represent it, have finally gotten the memo that says criticism of BLM is really stupid. We hate the word 'stupid', but all that the criticism has done is fan the fire. The criticism boiled down to: 'we are the police; we have the power and some people who happened to be black were wrongly shot and killed because they were bad guys. They may have been innocent people, at least when they were shot, but they are bad guys because we say they are.'

It does appear in large part this rhetoric is now history. We say in large part because there will always be someone who says something stupid. Then, there will always be mistakes made, there will always be a wrong decision made by someone, and we suggest the likelihood is high there will always be a young, unarmed black man who will do something foolish at the wrong time and get himself shot by a police officer. But departments are making the effort to improve training for officers to better serve all citizens. Training has always focused on the protection of the officer and little has centered on the interactions between the officer and citizens. Instruction, rightfully so, will continue to focus on officer and citizen protection, but a new emphasis is emerging to bring an awareness to officers of acting in a way that will cause the least harm to others.

You will not find a directive in any recognized training manual in American policing that instructs an officer to kick, punch, bash, batter, pummel, crush, maul or beat a subject into submission. This would only be permissible if the officer was fighting for his or her life. However, you will find many instances of failed training, the acceptance of poor behavior by other officers and outrageously negligent supervision. Surprisingly, this still occurs after years of news coverage decrying the actions, decades of pleas by offended citizens, protest riots, the creation of the BLM movement and of officers being indicted, some convicted of the illegal use of force and worse. Saving the best for last, the illegal use of force still occurs even though it is common knowledge that video cameras of all sorts seem to be everywhere. The proliferation of video has made the likelihood of officer misconduct being made public extremely high (Franklin & Hein, personal communication, 2018).

No one knows what an officer feels or is thinking when unnecessary force is used. The officer may not even know. However, it is apparent officers are apprehensive when interacting with some in society who seemingly have no respect for authority, their life or the lives of others. From experience we know an officer does have respect for life and authority and is focused on enforcing the law and maintaining order. We know the apprehension an officer feels can cause anxiety during an enforcement action that creates a focus so great that an officer can act too quickly without understanding the risk to him or herself and others. An officer can become careless and lose awareness of his or her surroundings. The knowledge of video should have a calming affect but certainly does not because of this focus (Franklin & Hein, personal communication, 2018).

Some departments are energizing community policing where officers are more than encouraged to get to know the citizens they serve and work with individuals and groups to reduce crime and make life better for both officers and citizens. In late 2017, the Duluth, Minnesota department began what they call 'customer service' training. Chief Mike Tusken said, "We're really good about training officers to be tactically sound—to have good critical-thinking skills and decision-making. . . . But one of the areas we can improve upon is soft skills. Better communication will enhance your perspective and the way you look at problem-solving" (Olsen, 2017). The department is collaborating with Dale Carnegie Training to develop a tweaked version for law enforcement of the "organization's standard 24-hour 'Skills for Success' course" (Olsen, 2017) normally given to business executives.

"Ultimately, when I think of Dale Carnegie, I think of customer service," Tusken said. "So many times it's used in industry, and policing really is about customer service. For years, it wasn't always looked at like that. We're a monopoly. You don't get to pick another police department because you don't like Duluth. So we always have to be at our best" (Olsen, 2017).

In New York City the police are revitalizing their community policing strategy to improve "communication and collaboration between local police officers and community residents. . . . The NYPD has long encouraged officers to strengthen bonds with the communities they patrol, but past practice in precincts left little time or opportunity for true community engagement. In recent years, the Patrol Services Bureau has systematically reorganized its patrol methods to achieve the goal of establishing Neighborhood Policing in every precinct, citywide, by 2019" (NYPD, 2018). Chief of Patrol Rodney Harrison stated, "We have more police officers on the streets who are in the process of building relationships," said Harrison. "Having that shared responsibility with the residents of the city of New York, that's a great way of being able to maintain violence at a low level" (NYPD, 2018). New York Police Department Commissioner James O'Neill wants to build a sense of unity in the city and make officers an integral part of citizens' lives. In addition, in early 2018, NYPD announced it would initiate implicit bias training for all uniformed officers (DaSilva, 2018).

Chicago superintendent Eddie Johnson stated: "The Chicago Police Department is on the road to reform. For nearly two years, CPD has worked with Chicagoans, our members, national experts, and police departments across the country to develop a series of best practices that will allow us to make this Department better for everyone. Making CPD better will mean safer streets, safer police officers, and stronger community trust through professionalism, accountability, and transparency to those we serve" (CPD, 2018). The department has implemented an overall plan to transform itself through training, supervision and leadership that will better serve the community. To be transparent, these reforms were developed because of the investigation of the department by the U.S. Department of Justice. A report issued by the department and the United States Attorney's Office, Northern District of Illinois, dated January 13, 2017, outlined egregious errors of judgment in use of force, lapses in accountability of actions, deficiencies in training, failures in supervision and other areas that needed improvement (U.S. Department of Justice, 2017).

As reported in *American Police Beat* (APB) in March 2019, a federal judge approved plans bringing major changes to Chicago Police Department operations. Additional funding is being given for increased focus on community policing, mental health support and counseling, crisis intervention and guidance on interactions with transgender individuals and people with disabilities. Changes have also been made to use of force policies. However, as reported in *APB,* former Attorney General Jeff Sessions called the plan a 'colossal mistake' (American Police Beat, 2019).

Not surprisingly, on October 10, 2018, prior to its approval, the *Associated Press* reported the Trump administration was opposing the reform plan. After the city ended talks with the U.S. Justice Department it developed a plan with the State of Illinois. It appears partisan politics is alive and well as Democratic Chicago clashes with a Republican administration. The Trump administration is not a fan of consent decrees because they "can unfairly malign officers," while Chicago officials believe the administration is out of step with citizen desires and out of touch with reality (Tarm, 2018)

Other new age training that many departments are introducing include understanding implied bias, interactions with the mentally ill, scenario-based use of force, intercommunications skills and many other training options. Training in such areas as de-escalation of incidents, the proper use of Tasers and crisis intervention are also being introduced or training hours increased. These improvements, however, do not mean we are all entering utopia.

In early 2019, the city of Cincinnati decided to introduce legislation requiring mandatory bias sensitivity training, not only for police officers, but for all city employees. Body-cam videos show officers in two different incidents using foul language including the n-word while interacting with citizens in heated confrontations (Donaghue, 2019). The efforts for betterment continue even with individual officers.

Another new age effort, although seemingly short lived, is the lip-sync battles between police officers that are being created on social media. Officers lip-sync well known and, arguably, popular soft rock, club and other music genre. The dancing and singing officers are entertaining and memorable and show a side of American policing many have not seen before-a personal, softer side.

According to the New York Police Department's *Annual Use-of-Force Report,* 2017 saw the fewest police firearm discharges ever recorded in the city. There was a 28% decrease in total police discharge incidents from 2016. This is the lowest annual discharge total since 1971. The years 2015, 2016 and 2017 recorded the three lowest police firearm discharge totals since recordkeeping began in 1971 (NYPD, 2017). Reportedly, the 2016 change in the department's use-of-force policies have increased officer accountability and encouraged restraint. These statistics, of course, do not mitigate the death by police of Eric Garner on Staten Island in July 2014, or the disrespect and indignity shown to Jazmine Headley by police in Brooklyn in December 2018, for reportedly sitting on the floor of a public benefits office. Video shows police prying her infant from her arms during arrest.

NOT EVERYONE WANTS A CULTURE CHANGE

Remember we said it appeared in large part misguided rhetoric is now history? We misspoke. Now the rhetoric is not against BLM but between politicians and police unions. In April 2019, during his State of the City address, Mayor Jacob Frey stated Minneapolis police would no longer be allowed to participate in 'warrior training,' even off duty. Mayor Frey believes fear-based training teaches officers a mindset that is contrary to good policing. Others believe the training produces paranoia which increases the probability of the use of unnecessary force (Mannix, 2019).

"Chief Medaria Arradondo's police department rests on trust, accountability and professional service," Frey said. "Whereas fear-based, warrior-style trainings like killology* are in direct conflict with everything that our chief and I stand for in our police department. Fear-based trainings violate the values at the very heart of community policing. When you're conditioned to believe that every person encountered poses a threat to your existence, you simply cannot be expected to build out meaningful relationships with those same people" (Mannix, 2019).

---

*We understand the word killology was first used by retired U.S. Army Lt. Col Dave Grossman, in his book, *On Killing: The Psychological Cost of Learning to Kill in War and Society,* first published in 1996.

We are sure Mayor Frey's policy change has everything to do with the shooting of Justice Damond, a woman who called 9-1-1 to report a possible assault near her home. When Damond approached a police car, an officer believing her to be a threat fired one shot and killed her. The officer, in the same month of the mayor's address, was convicted of third-degree murder and manslaughter.

What the mayor said is true, at least we believe it so, but his presentation did not sit well with the police union. The mayor said it, not the police chief. Apparently, the union was not aware of the change or certainly is not in favor of it. Re-evaluating training, rather than excluding 'warrior' training, would have been received better by the union and might have saved the mayor from a confrontation. A military mindset is the cornerstone of a boisterous, insistent minority in American policing. The mayor gave the police union a new target for their intense anger of criticism. The mayor must understand many union members, whether in policing or the auto industry, may value their union more than their employer.

In response to Mayor Frey's proclamation, the Minneapolis police union announced it is offering free 'warrior-style' training to all comers. The free training will be offered only as long as the mayor holds office. This poke in the eye may speak volumes about the relationship the mayor has with the police union and may reveal the union's real opinion of 'warrior' training. In any event, the mayor seems to be offering an olive branch to offended citizens while the union seems to want to continue business as usual. To cover all the bases, while the union is offering 'warrior-style' training, reportedly the training also includes de-escalation training.

We recommend someone should tell the mayor 'warrior style' training should continue to be given to SWAT team members. We also believe the mayor should increase his knowledge of the police psyche. We suggest the majority of the department members would have no problem with what the mayor said if the mayor had a respectable association with the police union. The mayor is now working with an outspoken union representative who apparently will try his best to politically damage the mayor. While this soap opera plays out, it seems Chief Arradondo is staying on the sidelines (Franklin & Hein, personal communication, 2019).

In spite of lapses of proper conduct vigorously covered by the media and well-meaning politicians with a shallow understanding of law enforcement, most in American policing hear the cry of the masses. Now is the time for the black community to stop and listen, to come to the table and compromise, to stop circling the wagons and understand why some subcultures in the black community are ripe for criticism.

IS THERE EQUAL OPPORTUNITY?

Why are we talking about the poor when we started talking about black men being shot by police? Because the poor and marginally poor are the usual, but not always, likely victims of police excesses; just ask a number of NBA and NFL players or Philando Castile, a school district nutrition services supervisor. But many would say the poor, of all races, are the victims of many things. If they are victims, they are victims of discrimination, of exploitation by corporate America, drug dealers and politicians.

According to the Fishlinger Center for Public Policy Research, forty percent of the public feel they are extremely or very interested in helping to solve the problem of poverty in the United States. Most Americans believe poverty is the result of social structure, interactions between members of society, rather than from individual choices. Close to sixty percent of Americans believe the foundation for poverty is an unequal social order; approximately forty percent believe an individual's lack of effort is to blame for poverty. There is a division of opinion regarding the basis for poverty, depending upon political views and the sex and age of respondent. There is some argument that poverty is not being adequately addressed. The federal and state governments spend billions of dollars per year on poverty programs, and according to the Fishlinger Center only twenty-one percent of respondents believe poverty is being addressed to any real extent (Fishlinger Center for Public Policy Research, 2016). We already have learned that poverty has been reduced by government programs, but poverty still exists in double digits. Even as unemployment has fallen during the Trump administration, many would still say that although the economy continues to improve, there has been no real increase in the number of jobs paying a living wage. Many would say all that poor people want is just an opportunity, an equal opportunity.

SUCCESSES AND FAILURES

Almost anyone can avoid poverty and enter the mainstream of society without forfeiture of culture. However, while some understand how to grasp opportunities that present themselves, others do not. Still, poor choices create less than positive outcomes. Because of these choices, some opportunities do not afford entrance into the mainstream, but offer limited, unfavorable prospects. While many government support programs sustain people in poverty, most may not lift them out of it. Because of poverty and police misconduct, enter a new civil rights movement.

As you know, the Black Lives Matter movement has been a success in many ways. Negative police responses to criticism has abated, a military reply to civil disorder has been or is being reassessed and police training is being revised to better address societal ills. Corporate America, i.e. Starbucks, is more sensitive to public opinion and the possibility of disparaging people of color. Black Lives Matter, along with others, have changed certain aspects of society, but the changes are superficial and could very well be transient because efforts have not sufficiently addressed discrimination, bigotry or poverty. It is transient because without a continued effort, successes can digress.

On the national level, the Black Lives Matter movement is leaderless and to some degree has diluted its focus by joining with other organizations that make up the Movement for Black Lives. Many demands of the larger parent organization are unrealistic, idealistic and unworkable. Demands like reparations for the continuing harms of colonialism and slavery,* defunding certain elements of the criminal justice system, and, for those most impacted in black communities, to control the laws, institutions and policies to create a new world (Move for Black Lives, n.d.). The demands include solutions and action that should be taken by federal, state and city governments. It appears, however, the solutions and actions do not take into account the culture some intercity youths have, whether black or white. They also do not take into account the limitations of school officials because of political correctness, legal liabilities and the fact officials have an

---

*The subject of reparations for slavery was, again, discussed by politicians and political hopefuls. During the early 2020 Democratic primary debates, we suggest the subject is being discussed because the black vote is expected to play a powerful role in the next presidential election. We also suggest the payment of reparations is unlikely to succeed.

obligation to actually teach while trying to control well-known chaos in many schools.

Although some demands are well thought out and would be a model for any society the movement thought they were in a candy store and could sample anything they wanted. Many of the demands are delusions that may be a pleasure to think about, but are unlikely to be realized.

Successes can also come with failures; violent crime rates have been rising (or falling). Some believe many officers are afraid to police. In many areas of a city, particularly those with a sizeable minority population, it may be difficult to find a police presence. This is another example of the Ferguson effect which we intimated while discussing the riot in Charlottesville. The Ferguson effect was coined soon after Michael Brown was shot by police officer Darren Wilson in Ferguson, Missouri. The effect is a concept that promotes the belief heightened examination of police actions has caused police to disengage from aggressive policing. Officers believe reduced activity will decrease their exposure to criticism, harm and liability. But the creation of the Ferguson effect, if there is one, can be shared by police and a certain subculture of society and, of course, the Black Lives Matter movement.

There is a debate among academics whether there is de-policing-whether, in fact, there is a Ferguson effect. If a person with a weapon is truly determined to shoot someone, it will not matter how much patrol is occurring. There is so little respect for authority today that the determined will commit the act whether or not there is a periodic patrol presence. People who have a particular bent or grievance against others who have accessibility to firearms are only made more dangerous due to their lack of ability to control their anger. Even in hot spots where there is increased, focused police presence in usually small areas, there can be shootings because of gang activity. It seems strong police presence, at times, provokes some of the worst offenders. The fix cannot be accomplished by police alone.

THE FIX WOULD VIOLATE POLITICAL CORRECTNESS

A civil society is characterized by a set of standards, rules of right conduct and expectations that display respect, cooperation and a set of values that add worth to society. There is a certain subculture that includes some who are not in the mainstream, with others only on the fringe, who exhibit an attitude that violates values of mainstream society. Many members of this subculture violate criminal laws, cause disorder, injury and fear. Others merely display disregard for fundamental principles and show, through their interactions, disrespect to conventional society. It seems Bill Cosby, during his rant, may have been speaking of this very subculture that lacks mainstream standards, rules and expectations.

Many will not agree, but the poor are not being well represented-the poor of any color. Are people of color discriminated against? Are there whites who are afraid of and bigoted against blacks? Out of frustration are there blacks who return the discontent to others? Of course, but without concessions, business as usual will continue. There are too many agendas, but there can only be one. But some do not want to hear the truth. As James Comey stated, "Ethical leaders choose a higher loyalty to those core values over their own personal gain" (Comey, 2018). There is a higher loyalty to the truth. But there are bullies; we all hear about bullies in the news every day—bullies who want their way. Bill Cosby was bullied because others could not accept what mainstream society believed is the truth. Bill Cosby was bullied because others who believed as he did were afraid to step up. There was a disservice to the black community and especially to the poor who want the opportunity to better themselves. The country must fix its errors, but there must be a consensus. Is anyone listening or is everyone just talking?

Everyone has principles-some not as honorable as others. Everyone has a guiding sense of conduct or an opinion or an understanding by which their actions are derived. These principles guide one's decisions on every topic, and a principled person may not want to make a detour no matter the consequence. But there is something called principled compromise. Many civil rights activists and many members of Congress do not believe it. They would rather have no compromise and continue business as usual than give an inch. We believe, however, there is principled compromise. There must be or nothing gets accomplished. Are the poor also victims? Yes, they are! Are people discriminated against? Yes, they are! Are family structures failing because of irresponsible parents, drugs, the likelihood of a poor education and unwise priorities? Yes, they are! Now that we all are in agreement, let's move forward and solve these problems. We all know it is not as easy as that, and most do not understand that the issue is not just a domestic one.

WE ARE NOT ALONE

No matter what one's opinion or judgment of race relations, the plight of the poor or the actions of the Black Lives Matter movement, our domestic ills are reportedly being encouraged and enflamed by a long-time foreign enemy. Prior to the 2016 presidential election U.S. intelligence agencies were aware of Russian interference in the national electoral process. Reportedly, the Russian government directed by Vladimir Putin, interfered with the 2016 presidential election to offer favor to their preferred candidate, Donald Trump. The Russians also reportedly wanted to discredit and prevent Hillary Clinton from winning the election. The Committee to Investigate Russia, a non-profit, purportedly bipartisan resource to help Americans recognize Russia's attacks on our democracy states, ". . . we do know creating and disseminating false information is a weapon of political warfare the Soviet Union and Russia have been using for decades" (Committee to Investigate Russia, 2017).

As reported by CNN, studies commissioned by the [United States] Senate Intelligence Committee detailed how the Russian state-supported Internet Research Agency (IRA) used voter-suppression techniques to quell black voter turnout and fearmongering to energize Republican voters. The IRA capitalized on black anger over racial inequities and moved blacks to reject the election or pursue faulty voting procedures. Reportedly, black voter turnout declined for the first time in 20 years for the 2016 presidential election (Love, 2018).

In September 2017, Facebook Security reported that the social network sold tens of thousands of dollars of ads to what turned out to be unauthentic accounts that all originated in Russia. Facebook "representatives indicated the ads focused on divisive issues such as race relations and polarizing topics such as the Second Amendment right to bear arms. The ads likely targeted swing state voters, but even without political campaign precision, they would have advanced the Kremlin aim of weakening democracy, in part by turning Americans against one another" (Committee to Investigate Russia, 2017). An objective of Putin's strategy is to globally undermine democracies—

". . . the ones with the greatest ability to affect his domestic political and economic status and impact Russia's foreign policy" (Committee to Investigate Russia, 2017).

According to the Gerasimov Doctrine as reported by Molly McKew in *Politico Magazine:* "Chaos is the strategy the Kremlin pursues: Gerasimov specifies that the objective is to achieve an environment of permanent unrest and conflict within an enemy state. . . . Thanks to the internet and social media, the kinds of operations Soviet psy-ops [psychological operations] teams once could only fantasize about—upending the domestic affairs of nations with information alone—are now plausible" (McKew, 2017).

General Valery Gerasimov is the chief of the General Staff of Russia's military. In February 2013, he published an article in the Russian trade paper, *Military-Industrial Kurier. In the article, The Value of Science is in the Foresight,* he discussed the Gerasimov Doctrine, the blending of long-held Soviet tactics along with strategic military thinking that promotes indirect aggression against an enemy society rather than a head-on attack. As Molly McKew reported, General Gerasimov believes "The role of nonmilitary means of achieving political and strategic goals has grown, and, in many cases, they have exceeded the power of force of weapons in their effectiveness" (McKew, 2017).

According to documents reviewed by NBC News as recently as 2018, Russians have been linked to arousing unrest and violence in the United States. The documents reportedly summarized a plan to influence and radicalize U.S. blacks and exploit racial tensions. Evidence reviewed suggests that Russians believe the election of Donald Trump as president of the United States has stirred racial conflicts in American society and that the project would threaten our unity and military and economic potential (Engel, et al., 2019).

In early 2020, congressional house members were warned Russia is continuing to interference with the 2020 election (Goldman et al., 2020). Reportedly, Russia was helping Bernie Sanders to be the democratic contender against President Trump. We now know the attempt failed, but it is Russia's intent to cause as much chaos as possible to undermine our democracy and to keep Donald J. Trump, known by many as the 'great divider', as the president of the United States.

In April 2020, CNN reported President Trump and Russian President Vladimir Putin appear to have had more sustained contact with each other in a recent two-week period than at any time since 2016. "Reaching out to the United States . . . is part of Putin's long-term plan to basically undermine the credibility of the United States as an important stalwart player in the global system, to undermine our alliances, and then to create as many lasting sources of tension be-tween Donald Trump and his own national security team," [Andrew] Weiss [a vice president for studies at the Carnegie Endowment for International Peace] told CNN. "The more that Russia succeeds in doing that, the less pressure Russia itself is likely to face from a uni-fied western camp" (Gaouetter et al., 2020).

Russian efforts to disrupt American democracy adds a new dynamic to our domestic ills and the various calls for culture change. Now is the time for all in American society to move the chairs closer to the table of compromise.

REFERENCES

American Police Beat. (2019). Judge oks "needed reforms" for Chicago Police Department. Los Angeles, CA. *xxxvi*(3), 1, 21.

Bauder, D. (2020). CBS News head calls threats against Gayle King reprehensible. *AP News*. https://apnews.com/1b8a3ad60aa2728fa721fb69e4af4b63

Bunn, C. (2020). Black health experts say surgeon general's comments reflect lack of awareness of black community. *NBC News*. https://www.nbcnews.com/news/nbcblk/black-health-experts-say-surgeon-general-s-comments-reflect-lack-n1183711x

Cherry, K. (2018). Uninvolved parenting: characteristics, effects, and causes. *verywellmind*. https://www.verywellmind.com/what-is-uninvolved-parenting-2794958

Chicago Police Department. (2018). A better CPD for everyone. https://home.chicagopolice.org/office-of-reform-management/

College of Mount Saint Vincent. (2016). *Society of the individual: root causes of poverty in America*. Fishlinger Center for Public Policy Research. https://mountsaintvincent.edu/society-or-the-individual-root-causes-of-poverty-in america/

Comey, J. (2018). *A higher loyalty: Truth, lies, and leadership*. New York, NY: Flatiron Books, pp. xi, 141–142.

Committee to Investigate Russia. (2017). How Russia operates. https://investigaterussia.org/how-russia-operates

Da Silva, C. (2018). NYPD will launch implicit bias training for police officers three years after Eric Garner's death. Newsweek. http://www.newsweek.com/nypd-start-implicit-bias-training-three-years-after-eric-garners-death-790248

Digital Library of Georgia. (2013). Civil Rights Digital Library. *Watts riots*. http://crdl.usg.edu/events/watts_riots/?Welcome

Donaghue, E. (2019). Cincinnati mayor pushes for bias training after two officers use racial slurs during calls. *CBS News.* https://www.cbsnews.com/news/cincinnati -mayor-john-cranley-pushes-for-bias-training-after-two-officers-use-racial-slurs -during-calls/

Dyson, M. E. (2005). *Is Bill Cosby right? or has the black middle class lost its mind?* New York, NY: Basic Civitas Books.

Engle, R., Benyon-Tinker, K., & Warner, K. (2019). *Russian documents reveal desire to sow racial discord—and violence—in the US.* https://www.nbcnews.com/news/world /russian-documents-reveal-desire-sow-racial-discord-violence-u-s-n1008051

Gaouetter, N., Cohen, M., & Conte, M. (2020). Putin leverages coronavirus chaos to make a direct play to Trump. *CNN News.* https://www.cnn.com/2020/04/18 /politics/trump-putin-unprecedented-contacts/index.html

Geary, D. (2015). Moynihan report: an annotated edition. a historian unpacks the Negro family: the case for national action on its 50th anniversary. *The Atlantic.* https://www.theatlantic.com/politics/archive/2015/09/the-moynihan-report -anannotated edition/404632/

Goldman, A., Barnes, J., Haberman, M., & Fandos, N. (2020). Lawmakers are warned that Russia is meddling to re-elect Trump. *The New York Times.* https: //www.nytimes.com/2020/02/20/us/politics/russian-interference-trump-democrats .html

Haskins, R. (2009). *The sequence of personal responsibility.* Washinggton, DC: The Brookings Institution. https://www.brookings.edu/articles/the-sequence-of -personal-responsibility/

Johnson, L. B. (1964). January 8, 1964: State of the Union. *Miller Center. University of Virginia.* https://millercenter.org/the-presidency/presidential-speeches/january -8-1964-state-union

Love, D. A. (2018). Russia's targeting of black voters is a very American thing to do. *Cable News Network.* https://www.cnn.com/2018/12/19/opinions/senate-reports -russia-facebook-2016-election-and-race-david-love/index.html

Law.com (2020). *Parental neglect.* https://dictionary.law.com/Default.aspx?selected =1446

Olsen, T. (2017). Duluth police recruits will test 'customer service' training. *Duluth News Tribune.* https://www.policeone.com/police-training/articles/461444006 -Minn-police-department-to-provide-customer-service-training-to-new-recruits/

Mannix, A. (2019). Minneapolis to ban 'warrior' training for police Mayor Jacob Frey says. *Star Tribune.* http://www.startribune.com/minneapolis-to-ban-warrior -training-for-police/508756392/

Matthews, D. (2012). Poverty in the 50 years since 'the other America,' in five charts. *The Washington Post.* https://www.washingtonpost.com/news/wonk/wp/2012/07 /11/poverty-in-the-50-years-since-the-other-america-in-five-charts/?utm_term =.a72b80a47da3

McKew, M. K. (2017). The Gerasimov Doctrine: it's Russia's new chaos theory of political warfare. And it's probably being used on you. *Politico Magazine.* https: //www.politico.com/magazine/story/2017/09/05/gerasimov-doctrine-russia -foreign- policy-215538

Move for Black Lives. (n.d.). *Platform.* https://policy.m4bl.org/platform/

New York City Police Department. (2017). *2017 use of force report.* https://www1.nyc
.gov/assets/nypd/downloads/pdf/use-of-force/use-of-force-2017.pdf

New York City Police Department. (2018). *Neighborhood policing.* https://www1.nyc
.gov/site/nypd/bureaus/patrol/neighborhood-coordination- officers.page

Sewer, A. (2015). Bill Cosby's famous "pound cake" speech, annotated. *BuzzFeed
News.* https://www.buzzfeednews.com/article/adamserwer/bill-cosby-pound-for
-pound

Sisario, B., & Sperling, N. (2020). Pressure by Simmons over exposé, Oprah Winfrey
faced a big decision. *The New York Times.* https://www.nytimes.com/2020
/01/17/movies/oprah-winfrey-russell-simmons-movie.html

Tarm, M. (2018). Trump administration opposes Chicago police reform plan. *Associated Press.* https://www.apnews.com/36187d7582a84eb6b4b4e542985aba29

University of California, Davis. (2017). Center for Poverty Research. *Current estimates
of poverty in the U.S.* https://poverty.ucdavis.edu/faq/what-current-poverty-rate
-united-states

U.S. Census Bureau. (2017). Income and Poverty in the United States: 2016. *People
and family in poverty by selected characteristics: 2015 and 2016 [table 3].* https:
//www.census.gov/library/publications/2017/demo/p60-259.html

U.S. Department of Justice, Civil Rights Division and United States Attorney's
Office Northern District of Illinois. (2017). *Investigation of the Chicago Police
Department.* https://www.justice.gov/opa/file/925846/download

Yen, H. (2019). AP Fact Check. Trump exaggerates his role in black job gains. *AP
News.* https://apnews.com/f78f4205f474482db8bb8fa7a5ebfa27

Chapter Nine

WE OFFER NO APOLOGY

Leadership has a harder job to do than just choose sides. It must bring sides together.

Jessie Jackson, Sr.
Civil Rights Activist

Some might say the United States government has done more to liberate people elsewhere in the world than it has in our own country. However, a government can only do so much. Many in the United States have failed to understand opportunities presented to them and still consider themselves victims. Others around the world have recognized opportunities and seized them. But, as in many parts of the world, there is still exploitation of the American black community, both from within and by mainstream society. Although American policing is part of mainstream society, it is limited to what can be changed for the betterment of any community. For that betterment, however, major changes to police culture are on the horizon. Although limited, some changes have arrived, and others are coming that will focus on how the enforcement of law and the maintenance of order is administered.

Over time, civil rights movements have successfully been the vanguard in changing police policies to end physical and psychological exploitation. In recent years, because of 21st century attempts to solve one of society's many ills, American policing has accepted that cultural change is needed and is striving to remake street officers and supervisors into new-century police. The black community is facing an opportunity and must look it in the eye, but first the black community must understand that political correctness can marginalize success.

145

THE BACKLASH OF POLITICAL CORRECTNESS

The title of this chapter might cause concern for some readers. Some might say we are racist because of what we have written, but judgments at times are wrong. Being a fiscal conservative does not make one a member of the Republican Party. Believing in global warming does not make one a member of the Democratic Party. Not all gun owners belong to the NRA. Anyone who has not lived in a closet for the last 40 years knows that political correctness is a term that describes almost anything that avoids insult, discrimination, or even the perception of discrimination of people because of gender, sexual orientation or race. It can be the avoidance of a "look," a statement or action. Political correctness has helped to level the playing field and has helped to redress an imbalance. The avoidance of certain speech and actions has made life for many in the black community more bearable. What has become known as political correctness has allowed many in the white community to have a greater understanding of varying cultures. We support political correctness, but taken to an extreme it can create insensitivity and a sense of uncaring. Political correctness can prevent injustice, but it can also cause national security threats and community indifference. Political correctness can cause a false sense of wellness, apathy, alienation, and hostility. It can cause an unwanted separation of people. Can our borders be secure when rational thought is overtaken by sympathy and pity? Can society help the disadvantaged when a culture cannot be criticized for disrespect and crime? Is a rush to judgment causing a bitterness that is dividing us?

Political correctness entered a new dimension in recent years when Harvey Weinstein, a former Hollywood film producer, was accused of sexual misconduct by numerous women. The #MeToo movement, an action against sexual assault among other things, reportedly was given a considerable boost by social media immediately after allegations surfaced of wrongdoing by Weinstein.

The #MeToo movement has frightened some offending men and empowered some women. However, it has also created a backlash that may be creating a situation that will reverse many gains by women. In early December 2018, Bloomberg (Tan & Porzecanski, 2018) reported the squawk on Wall Street was that many in the financial sector were beginning to back away from women. One financial adviser said just hiring a woman creates an unknown risk. Reportedly, men are avoiding being alone with women to prevent a situation where they can be accused of wrongdoing. We do not minimize the seriousness of sexual harassment or assault, but the movement has created a political correctness on steroids which makes the mere suspicion of inappropriate sexual contact a career-ending supposition. For corporate America, there seems to be a rush to judgment to avoid insult with no recognized due process when accused of sexual misconduct. It is politically incorrect to harass or assault women and politically correct to distance oneself from a violator.

Kevin Hart, a black man, knows political correctness can also be unforgiving. The comedian was slated to host the 2019 Academy Awards. Two days after the announcement he stepped down because of controversy caused by his disparaging remarks about the LGBTQ community on Twitter made seven years earlier. Hart actually disqualified himself reportedly because of embarrassment and for disappointing his peers. Ellen DeGeneres, a self-outed lesbian, gave Hart her support to be reinstated as the awards host but was criticized for her efforts (Shoard, 2019). Verbally or physically attacking others is no longer accepted by mainstream society, and other celebrities like film director James Gunn and comedian Roseanne Barr have lost lucrative contracts, and many others are feeling the heat (Levine, 2018). Conversely, certain parts of the black community are neglected because of political correctness that mandates no criticism can be given.

Political correctness discourages discourse; it discourages problem solving, at least in the black community. Problems exist in some black communities not only because of racism and inherent discrimination, but because one would not dare criticize black culture in an effort to effectively deal with historic and deeply rooted problems. To violate PC would only intensify the resistance to criticism shown by black pundits. Political correctness, or the lack of it, can cause unintended consequences—just ask Bill Cosby.

For decades, the pendulum controlling the rights and wrongs of the black community has been idle, siding with a few pundits whose chosen avocation is to defend black culture no matter the cost. The problem we see is that the cost is borne largely by the black community. There are many in the community who do many things to direct boys and girls and young men and women to act responsibly and enter the mainstream (don't forget the celebration of Kwanzaa we have already mentioned, but there is also the BMe Community, Uniquely You Summit, Girl Up, The YBM Leadership Alliance, My Brother's Keeper, Common Ground Foundation, Teaching for Change and many others), but there are others who are satisfied with the existing circumstances of hardship and sadness. While mothers scream that black-on-black or blue-on-black killing must stop, nothing changes because accepted authority dictates that disrespect, crime, the lack of discipline and unaccountability are caused by discrimination and that the community is powerless to address many of its ills. Political correctness has caused a type of backlash that stymies any attempts to improve the lives of many. It is politically correct to oppose and confront attitudes, speech and actions which demean, show bias, harass or violate one's person, but it is politically incorrect to rescue a subset of society from a corrupt culture because the effort would be considered critical, demeaning and racist.

We believe political correctness has gotten out of control. In late 2018, several radio stations stopped playing the 1944 song "Baby, It's Cold Outside" because of the belief the song presented a scenario of sexual assault. In 1949, the song achieved wide recognition when it was sung in the film, *Neptune's Daughter*. The film portrays a man plying a woman with drinks while she repeatedly says she wants to go home and he pleads not to leave because, baby, it's cold outside (Held, 2018). The song was written in a more innocent time when a man and woman were allowed to flirt without 21st century repercussions. In tandem, People for Ethical Treatment of Animals, commonly called, PETA, compared idioms like 'bringing home the bacon' or 'beat a dead horse' to homophobia and racism (Tara, 2018). It seems political correctness is out of control because it is about control.

We are not racist, but we are bold enough to tell it like it is, where conditions dictate that someone must do so. Pundits may find us to be disrespectful and insulting. We are politically incorrect at times because someone has to be to make a difference. Persons perceived as offending the black community do not get sympathy, even though they should not all be lumped into the single category of "racist." Sometimes constructive criticism is just that; it should initiate dialogue and lasting positive change. Change will not occur without judgment. We do not expect any sympathy from pundits for what we have said, but neither should young black men for disrespect shown among themselves or to others.

CRYING BABIES GET SYMPATHY

The federal government's policy of separating children from their parents when detained for illegally entering the United States caused a firestorm of indignation. The policy is long-standing but was brought to media attention when the U. S. Justice Department under the Trump administration changed enforcement policy to arrest and criminally prosecute adults who enter the United States illegally. Prior to the policy change, illegal immigrants when caught were released after receiving a scheduled hearing date.

There is no question separating children from their parents can cause panic and terror to both the child and parent. Several pundits exclaimed caging children is not who we are. After several weeks of demonstrations and political posturing, President Trump signed an executive order ending the practice, although anyone who stays up with current events knows the practice was never ended. However, the controversy was straightforward and politically addressed quickly—at least quickly in terms of the usual speed of national political actions. There was nothing politically incorrect about showing concern for a child's welfare. In fact, it was hoped that being politically correct solved the dispute. However, as reported in the media, as more and more immigrants have attempted to enter the country, thousands more children have been taken into custody by border protection forces.

Adults arrested for any crime, whether illegal immigrants entering the United States or a citizen committing any crime in the U.S., are separated from their children when jailed. If the children are with a U.S. citizen parent when arrested, the children may be released to a relative or may be placed in temporary custody for their protection and care until a more appropriate guardian is identified. We know of no jail facility that is designed to house both parents and children, although the federal government may now be housing families together. By 2019, however, thousands of children were still being separated from their parents, although federal officials state the separation has nothing to do with zero tolerance of illegal border crossing but, rather, the enforcement of existing federal law. When the 'catch and release' policy was changed to the arrest of illegal immigrants as they crossed the border, it was obvious to us that the Border Patrol, Immigration and Customs Enforcement agencies were not prepared to jointly house family units. What caused further controversy is the fact that not all children were accompanied by parents or adult family members. A large number of children were being smuggled by human traffickers, commonly called coyote smugglers. Our borders do need to be more secure, but we do not endorse President Trump's unorthodox statements and conduct or the way he is attempting to fund the construction of a $5 billion border wall (Franklin & Hein, personal communication, 2019).

The dynamics between being politically correct and incorrect can cause insurmountable difficulties when discussing what is best for the public good. American policing is politically correct in their efforts to correct wrongs made possible by inadequate training and poor supervision. It is also politically correct to address biases shown by officers. Frankly, many officers do not and will not understand their bias until they learn, through education, how attitude, remarks and actions exhibit insensitive, biased behavior.

There are moral and goodwill issues in both public outcries—an outcry for the welfare of innocent children and an outcry for the lives of black men. There are the lives of minority children, some of whom are too young to understand circumstances. Then there are the lives of young black men who are perceived to be criminal or at least disrespectful. Whether true or not, whether politically correct or not, there is a subculture within the black community that does not receive as much concern as crying children.

CRYING BABIES GET ACTION

A raging controversy sparked by pictures of crying children and agonized parents quickly changed the political posture in mid-2018 from border security and illegal immigration to social injustice. Presidential and congressional priorities change with the wind and political contributions. The most important news story of the day was not U.S. citizens losing health care, not terrorism, not the Russians interfering with our 2016 national elections. It was the separation of children from parents who committed a crime. Crying babies and grieving parents, albeit illegal immigrants, beat news footage of black youths being killed by police or burning buildings and turning over cars in response to the killing of Michael Brown or dozens of others.

Black youth killed by police, whether criminal or guiltless, arouses little consequence in mainstream society. The June 2018 shooting of Antwon Rose—another questionable shooting of a black youth—has gathered some but sparse attention. It's time to take a seat.

RIOTING YOUNG BLACKS GET ARRESTED

Rioting is not the best way to obtain concessions from others. Most disturbances have not garnered sympathy, but outrage. However, over the long haul public disorder has had some successes. In fact, in recent history, riots across the country in response to the wanton killing of black men have served to awaken police leaders to hasten reforms. But, for society to go forward, to make a greater effort in righting wrongs, to provide tailored assistance to the poor, the black community and their spokespersons must step up and do their part. As we stated, there are many efforts to educate the young, boys and girls, to enter the mainstream, but it is apparent not enough effort is focused on older adolescent and young adults to stop the disrespect and shooting.

As reported by William Lee in the *Chicago Tribune,* "There are good and bad in every profession, any profession, and I don't deny we have bad cops," said a black veteran patrol officer assigned to the majority black Wentworth [Chicago] police district on the South Side who asked not to be identified. "But what offends me the most is the protests like they're doing now. A possibly bad shooting happens somewhere else in the country—where is your protest over the 4-year-old who was just shot?"

"There are things to protest, but you attack us instead of attacking the actions of the gangbangers that you know, the people that you know have the guns," he said. "You know who shot the child, who robbed the old man, and you say nothing" (Lee, 2016).

The part to be played by black leadership might be a gargantuan task, almost impossible to achieve, but try they must. To take a place at the table, an effort must be made to reverse a subculture of crime and disrespect that is decades or more old. Political correcteness is hurting the black community—leaders have a fear of criticism from others, but a seat at the table means power.

NO LEADERSHIP, NO SEAT AT THE TABLE

In July 2018, Chicago Police shot and killed a barber, Harith Augustus, when he reached for a loaded, unlawfully carried gun as he was being pursued by several uniformed officers. An officer's body camera released within hours of the shooting clearly shows Augustus carrying a semi-automatic pistol. The video also clearly shows the barber reaching for the weapon when he was surrounded by police. Let us be clear here: Harith's own unwise move caused his death. Neighbors and friends soon rioted demanding justice. It did not seem the rioters cared that the video was clear and the shooting was deemed justified and little was accomplished. Little was gained by demonstrating or demanding that then Chicago Mayor Rahm Emanuel and then Chicago Police Superintendent Eddie Johnson resign when it seemed justice had been rightly served. This seemed to be a good time for black leadership in Chicago to show its strength within the black community, even to make it a 'teaching moment' about what not to do when confronted by police; yet none was forthcoming. Where was the city council member who wanted the extra police presence to address crime in the area where the shooting occurred? Why is the seat at the table still empty?

RESPONSIBILITY IS A THREE-WAY PLAY

There are three seats at the table. One is already taken by police leaders, but two are empty—one for activists and another for politicians. Although American policing has taken the most recent steps to repair racial injustice, responsibility for further advancements must be shared. A unilateral power play, using actions and information against others, only continues centuries-old political maneuvers. The police are in the midst of an awakening, to some extent activists are still in denial and politicians are, well, politicians. When something goes right, when a problem is solved, politicians will blast their image and self-aggrandizement on every television channel that will give the time. When things turn left instead of right, politicians are skillful at turning a blind eye or changing the subject and talking about the weather. As we say this, the death of George Floyd may go down in history as a major turning point in the American civil rights movement. As the world watched George Floyd die, new age politicians with a 21st century emphasis on social justice may be overtaking traditional politics. However, as the world continues to watch the transformation, we still must contend with age-old politics.

The actions of Chicago Mayor Rahm Emanuel is an example of politics not helping. As discussed previously, the shooting of Laquan McDonald in October 2014, by Chicago Police Officer Jason Van Dyke, was another questionable killing of a black man. Van Dyke shot McDonald 16 times within seconds of arriving on the scene. Although McDonald had a knife, was threatening and acting erratically, other officers already on the scene were still assessing the situation and no one else fired a shot. A Chicago police detective filed reports explaining the incident as a justifiable use of force. The final report was approved by a string of supervisors. Sometime later a dash cam video of the shooting was released, but only after a community outcry and a federal court order. The video could have been released immediately, but it was withheld from public view during the re-election campaign of Mayor Emanuel. The video appears to show that many of the 16 shots were fired while McDonald was lying on the ground facing away from Van Dyke. The video seems to contradict on-scene officer reports that McDonald lunged threateningly in the officer's direction. As we know, former officer Van Dyke was convicted by a jury of his peers and sentenced for second-degree murder.

As much controversy that was caused by the shooting of Laquan McDonald, the verdict caused little controversy. There was a demonstration to celebrate the guilty verdict, but there were no riots. The only anxiety seems to have been caused by the Fraternal Order of Police (FOP). The FOP disregarded video evidence and credible testimony by on-scene police officers and called the trial a sham and the jury verdict shameful. We are not partial to defense attorneys, but we must agree with one who said the verdict spoke volumes. The often used defense that an officer feared for his or her life is no longer the be-all end-all justification.

Let's not forget the officers indicted for obstruction of justice, conspiracy and official misconduct related to their complicity in publication of the alleged false initial report. We agree that the end is near for the old way of handling police business in Chicago that was shamefully put on full display for the entire world to see. In the past, all an officer had to say to end any further inquiry was, "I was placed in fear of my life." Cameras have changed all of this now, and yet there are still deep pockets of resistance to public accountability in the Chicago Police Department. What you saw in this trial are the last remnants of this resistance. Not many cops I know expected that Van Dyke would be convicted. That verdict was a huge shock to them, even to those who have acknowledged that Van Dyke screwed up. Most believed he would skate. I would like to say a new day of policing in Chicago is emerging, but we now know three officers charged for furthering a false report of the incident were found not guilty (Franklin, personal communication, 2019).

Not only did the shooting and untimely release of the dash cam video cause contention, but the prosecutor waited over a year to take action. In response to citizen demonstrations and indignation shown by city leaders, Mayor Emanuel fired Police Superintendent Garry McCarthy.

McCarthy was fired for four reasons:

1. The county prosecutor waited over one year to charge the officer with murder, but somehow McCarthy took the fall.
2. The mayor waited over one year to release the video to the public, but somehow McCarthy took the fall.
3. Politicians generally do not blame themselves for wrongdoing.
4. McCarthy, like many other police leaders, did not solve the problem of how to enforce culture change and strict policy adherence on street level officers.

As accountability in Chicago is still in question for both the police and politicians, the chief of the St. Paul, Minnesota police department took steps to ensure every officer under his leadership is aware of the high standards expected. In 2018, five St. Paul officers stood and watched as a former officer assaulted a civilian. Although it took a year to uncover and investigate the allegation, all five officers were fired for failing to follow professional standards and failing to intervene when a violent act occurred in their presence. Of course, the police union will contest the firings (Nelson & Furst, 2019).

As the tug of war between accountability and unacceptable behavior continues, politicians are still strutting around the table with a swagger trying to determine how to take a seat without losing their power, even the new age ones. Activists are still in denial; problems in the black community are caused by discrimination.

DOES A PRINCIPLED COMPROMISE
COMPROMISE PRINCIPLES?

Remember what we said about principled compromise and the fact it might violate political correctness. Representatives of the black community are absent from the table because principled compromise is not accepted. Compromise is not a surrender but a way to be effective. But acknowledgement of the disintegration of some parts of a subculture is not accepted. A police official once said if jewelry stores were being robbed, the police would not be watching sandwich shops but jewelry stores. Police focus on crime. If crime is in the black community, the police are active there. If blacks are incarcerated, it is because blacks commit crimes. We all know there is discrimination in the criminal justice system. Shouting from the rooftops that there is discrimination is not going to stop it, but compromise between the community and police will decrease it. Compromise is better than the stalemate that is ongoing. The worst thing a politician ever said was, "There will be no compromise!"

As a society we have an obligation to improve the lives of all people, even if they are not helping themselves. This is where the politicians take part. For further success, cooperation and a consensus is needed to stabilize public order and maintain an equilibrium for the public good. We believe racial strife is one of many dysfunctions in American society that can be decreased. Recent efforts to improve American policing have shown progress, but training and education is underfunded. Leaders on both sides of the aisle must share the effort for congressional support.

There are two things our national leaders are afraid of: the National Rifle Association (NRA) and losing their place at the congressional trough. Congressional members will not support gun control even though dozens of white youth are being killed in the classroom. If they will not save white children what are the chances they will make an effort to save black kids? A hope we see is the power of the polling place.

Many will say the black community is a community of democrats. Overall, that is most likely true, but 21st century blacks know that the Democratic Party is failing their community. The Republican Party is worse when representing blacks. Where is the indignation for poor blacks dropping out of school or graduating high school while being functionally illiterate? Or for those who are unemployed or being killed by overzealous police officers who too quickly shoot down a fleeing black youth?

We do not present ourselves as experts in political science or the chess game that is played in any political arena in which the goal is to win at whatever the cost. Therefore, we will not express our views at how votes should be cast or withheld. But there are maneuvers to be made that will place more of the black community in the mainstream of society. That is, of course, if the black elite will allow that.

I have always prided myself as being an independent thinker. I am neither a "yellow dog" Democrat nor a staunch Republican. When I first heard the phrase "yellow dog" Democrat I had to ask what it meant. I was surprised to be told that if the Democratic Party nominated a yellow dog for office, the person giving me the definition would vote for the yellow dog. I did not respond to the person because I did not want to offend. In 2020, the media reported that a voter mentioned he would rather vote for a tuna fish sandwich than the current president. It seems the yellow dog and tuna sandwich are closely related, but on different ends of the spectrum.

Along with priding myself as an independent thinker, as an idealist, I have always voted for the person, especially in a presidential race, who I thought would put the welfare of the country first. Although thinking as a realist, I know party politics and campaign fundraisers come first and not necessarily in that order. Of course, "yellow dog" Democrats and staunch Republicans would both say, the Democrat or the Republican candidate would do the most good for the country. What I have ended up doing for decades is voting for the person I thought was the lessor of two evils, although I have not always been right. So my swing vote is difficult to predict (Hein, personal communication, 2019).

The swing vote in the black community is dangerous for politicians and used to advantage might bring some unity to people of color. A swing voter cannot be counted on, but must be courted. But a swing voter is only one way of getting attention.

YOU HAVE OUR ATTENTION

As we have discussed, the demands of and demonstrations expressed by the black community in the 21st century are markedly different than was seen in the previous century. Likewise, police tactics are noticeably different and, in the early summer of 2020, are changing rapidly. There is an air of a new beginning. This time someone is listening. These changes can be readily seen on the nightly news.

There is also something that is decidedly different that seems to give black demonstrators a step up when being interviewed by television news journals—an air of approaching success. Although there has been some rioting, looting and property damage, that seems to be subsiding. The black demonstrators being interviewed are articulate and well spoken. They come with a purpose. They come not with a rage but with determination to accomplish a goal. They are not ones who are destroying but building. The demonstrators who are emerging are part of mainstream society who are expressing frustrations that all blacks feel because of the biased system in which they live. Demonstrations seem to have become more informative—still confrontational but less so. They are distinctly different from the angry mobs we all have seen in the past—the mobs which make the white community afraid.

There is also something that is decidedly different about police officers responding to the demonstrations; they are mostly tolerant, understanding, and sometimes friendly. We all have seen mistakes. One of the biggest caused the death of George Floyd. But we never thought we would see a police officer, a sergeant, a lieutenant, a chief with four stars on his collar kneeling in peace in support of demonstrators.

There is something else we noticed about the demonstrations in June 2020. Although we speak of black participants and the black spokespersons on television, an abundance of demonstrators were white. We hope this is an indication that demonstrations are promoting solidarity, and as a society we support and will help make constructive changes for those who just want equality.

As elected and pseudo leaders are failing to take a seat at the table, others are who are unafraid to take a stand. Local leaders are being replaced, or should we say, their job is being done by young and up-and-coming professionals and activists along with a handful in American policing who are not afraid to step up and step out of the norm.

This is all good and we hope it lasts, but efforts must be increased for true success—increased efforts to focus on the ones who rioted, who looted, who destroyed, and who ignored the rule of law. We are again speaking of that black subculture that must be saved from itself. Society, not just the black community, must make the ignorance of the rule of law and the rejection of the right standards of conduct a most shameful, humiliating and embarrassing concept. Society and the black community, not just American policing, must take part in the solution.

WHAT IS TO BE DONE?

It is common knowledge there is an abundance of firearms of all sorts in some black communities. This fact, along with many others, gives the police who are trying to be better guardians of the people and the law a sense of foreboding when interacting with or confronting people of color, particularly black males, in many neighborhoods. It is now time for the black community to take the next step if the gap between black communities and the police has any real hope of being bridged. The next step, the positive step to stop the degradation of the black community, is to acknowledge the ills, the hostility, and disorder everyone sees. It has never been hidden. To support the disadvantaged black community, pundits must ask how to decrease the number of blacks committing crimes rather than ask why more blacks are incarcerated than whites? Pundits must question how to fix dysfunctional families rather than claim that it is not the family structure but discrimination that is the cause of poverty, crime, disrespect, unemployment, and unstable families along with a multitude of other ills.

In her book, *Wouldn't Take Nothing for my Journey Now*, Maya Angelou writes, "Our youth, finding little or no courtesy at home, make exodus into streets filled with violent self-revulsion and an exploding vulgarity. We must re-create an attractive and caring attitude in our homes and in our worlds. If our children are to approve of themselves, they must see that we approve of ourselves. If we persist in self-disrespect and then ask our children to respect themselves, it is as if we break all their bones and then insist that they win Olympic gold medals for the hundred-yard dash. Outrageous." (Angelou, 1993).

Maya Angelou is notable for many things. She was a singer, dancer and civil rights activist. She is the author of seven autobiographies, several books of essays and poems, television shows, movies and plays. She was internationally recognized after her first autobiography, *I Know Why the Caged Bird Sings,* published in 1969. What brought her even more prominence was her recitation of her poem, "On the Pulse of Morning," at the inauguration ceremony of President Bill Clinton on January 20, 1993 (Franklin & Hein, personal communication, 2019).

As Associate Justice of the United States Supreme Court, Ruth Bader Ginsburg said, "Real change, enduring change, takes one step at a time" (Goodreads, 2019). It is time for the black community to take the next step, but what is the next step, what is the compromise?

Part of the compromise would be for the black community to acknowledge that certain aspects of black culture, parts which do not benefit the black community or any part of society, are not created, formed or generated solely by discrimination but by failures in black reality. A compromise would first recognize a significant portion in the black community uses self-harm to avoid the truth. This portion might be best known as "their own worst enemy." We express our rudimentary knowledge of psychology while we note our many years of watching portions of the black community operate in a self- destruct mode directly due to the lack of genuine engagement with dominant black leadership. Along with distant leadership, there could also be an arbitrary limitation in entering mainstream society created not only by white fear of blacks but because of a pervasive fear by many blacks that there is only so much room at the top. We are not asking for the destruction of black pride and culture. We are not encouraging any part of the black community to adopt white cultural traits. We understand that blacks have their own culture and pride and may never want to fully assimilate into what we call the mainstream of society. What we are saying is that any culture can and will emerge stronger without disrespect, a dysfunctional lifestyle or wanton killing which far too often leads to needless loss of life, particularly the lives of young black males.

I recently spoke to a white person who read this manuscript before it was published. He called it ignorant. There is no compromise there (Hein, personal communication, 2020). The man said when he speaks to others who believe there should be no compromise with bias he said many, both black and white, become emotional. He said, "blacks in the U.S. have had to endure racism for 400 years and they should not take any responsibility for their responses to it." He said the some-

times disrespectful and errant behavior exhibited by the black subculture discussed is all because of discrimination. "Some in the subculture who cannot protect themselves from discrimination act the
way they do because of their frustration with not being allowed to live
a life of freedom. A black neighborhood rife with violent black on
black crime, poverty and those who devalue education is caused by
discrimination." As do police, supporters of the rights of the black
community only hear what they want to hear (Hein, personal communication, 2020).

I told him I understand the history of racism in the U.S. and the
bias shown knowingly and implicitly by American policing. I support
the demonstrations caused by the death of George Floyd, but I vigorously oppose the stance that the black subculture and the entire black
community are not in some way responsible for black social ills. Black
social problems may be from discrimination, but to stop there without further action is absurd. It is right to demonstrate for liberty and
for fair and just treatment by American policing. I believe it is not
right to deny further exploration and demonstrate for a better life for
those who cannot help themselves. We must have compromise. I saw
some compromise on the nightly news when a number of black
demonstrators talked rioters out of criminally damaging property
(Hein, personal communication, 2020).

For those in the subculture to overcome discrimination, they must
show support for the demonstrations protesting bigotry and injustice.
They must work hard at showing respect to others to receive it themselves. As General Colin Powell said, "A dream does not become reality through magic; it takes sweat, determination, and hard work."
Many in the white community are afraid of all blacks because of a relatively few in a violent, disrespectful black subculture. There must be
a compromise among everyone in American society to right the
wrongs so many strive for (Hein, personal communication, 2020).

We do not discount the naiveté or implicit bias of television personality Megyn Kelly for saying in the past it was accepted for a white
person to be in black face. Clearly, Kelly is not alone in her belief.
There is much work to be done in the white community to understand
what it is like to hear and see words and images which denigrate people of color on a daily basis.

I became aware of contentious race relations sometime in the mid
to late 1950s while growing up on the south side of Chicago in West

Englewood. I never heard a disparaging remark from my parents but from neighborhood adults and children with whom I interacted. As the black community moved west around Ogden Park I began playing baseball with black kids my age, but not all relations were civil and several encounters were racially motivated. Because of my upbringing and the mentorship I received from many, I do not believe I was raised with bias. I have always shied away from others who exhibited racial hatreds (Hein, personal communication, 2020).

Although I do not believe I am biased, I do believe many in the white community do not understand how people in the black community think about respect and how bias shows disrespect. Many white people do not understand how comments and slights are perceived by black people. The unbiased thinking white community can actually be ignorant while believing they are being courteous to a black person when, in fact, one is actually being disrespectful. I am not offering an excuse. I am stating a fact. Many in the white community appear to be biased because they do not understand the historical significance or how the continued overt racism of the majority culture directly affects the black community. All in the white community who truly care about and are rethinking their own implicit or unconscious bias are being given a lesson in race relations while watching the nightly news (Hein, personal communication, 2019).

WILL THE PROSECUTION OF R. KELLY CHANGE THE BLACK COMMUNITY?

At the same time the white community is learning something meaningful, many in the black community seemingly ignore high profile black sports figures and entertainers who are assaulting women or promoting an unsafe, irresponsible lifestyle.

R. Kelly is the most egregious example of this malady (we are not forgetting Bill Cosby—he is already in jail). Over more than two decades the entertainer has allegedly debased and assaulted numerous black women and girls, and as we understand, much of the black community circled the wagons to protect him from justice. Many felt R. Kelly's rumored indiscretions were simply part of the entertainment business when one is a superstar, particularly a superstar of color. Reportedly, the exploitation was considered by many as salacious entertainment, not criminal behavior. R. Kelly is now, again, being prosecuted for sexual assault (Li et al., 2019).

There just is not enough caring. Much of the time caring is by the mother who has lost a child—shot by another, whether cop or civilian, black or white. For some, having a media personality or a politician apologize is a feel good power play that does not come close to solving the more serious ills of society. As so many have found, one dares not discuss race relations unless prepared to express regret, lose a livelihood, or be called not black enough. There certainly are athletes and celebrities who will step forward to help save the young if they knew there would be no repercussions.

As reported by CNN Sports: "Pretty much everything that [Michael] Jordan has touched turned to gold. His narrative is inspirational, his dedication almost impossible to rival and his enthusiasm infectious. . . . Jordan helped establish Chicago as a major player on the world sports map. Before his arrival in the summer of '84, the Bulls were known as the "traveling cocaine circus" and he didn't just clean up the team, he arguably helped clean up the city. . . . That city was fiercely divided on color lines, one of the hotbeds of prejudice in the country and Michael united people. . . . Everybody was a Bulls fan, no matter your political preference, [Dan] Roan, [WGN Chicago sports anchor], told CNN Sport. It didn't matter where you lived, it was kind of a galvanizing issue for the city. . . . While the Chicago native, former President Barack Obama, would have preferred Jordan to enter the political fray, he has some sympathy for his stance, saying in the film [*The Last Dance*]: 'America is very quick to embrace a Michael Jordan, an Oprah Winfrey or a Barack Obama, so long as it's understood that you don't get too controversial around broader issues of social justice'" (Riddell, 2020). Oops, we spoke too soon. The black elite cannot get involved in the broader issues of social justice like black men being killed at an alarming rate, poverty and bigotry. Remember, blacks must be sufficiently black.

IS THE TIME RIGHT FOR CHANGE?

'The Last Dance': The Untold Story of Michael Jordan's Chicago Bulls was broadcast during the heat of national demonstrations over the killing of George Floyd. Another attempt of racial conciliation was

ongoing, but something was different this time. Many examples of concessions by both demonstrators and police were evident on the nightly news. Police officers joined demonstrators and demonstrators confronted rioters who were destroying, not building. Over time, seemingly gathering strength among themselves, a number of city mayors began to speak out. Again, it was different this time. The mayors were not the typical old white guy city mayor, but a group of new-age mayors who might make a difference this time. A group of newly elected black, female city mayors began to speak out.

On a Friday in June in Atlanta, another black man was shot dead by police and, again, the frustrated voiced their feelings. But this time Atlanta Mayor Keisha Lance Bottoms said America will "get to the other side of this. . . . I think that while we are doing it [changing tactics and improving training] in our police departments *there is clearly a bigger conversation* [emphasis added by authors] that has to be had across the county because we are not in a post-racial society and the biases are still there" (LaBlanc, 2020).

Bottoms first received national attention when she denounced vandalism and said, "What I see happening on the streets of Atlanta is not Atlanta. This is not a protest. This is not in the spirit of Martin Luther King, Jr.," an impassioned Bottoms said at a news conference. "This is chaos" (LaBlanc, 2020).

Bottoms was one of four mayors from across the country participating in a CNN town hall discussing police shootings of black men and the ensuing demonstrations. This new racial consternation "has prompted the kind of soul searching . . . that many advocates have been urging for decades" (LaBlanc, 2020). This message was echoed by mayors Lori Lightfoot of Chicago, London Breed of San Francisco and Muriel Bowser of Washington, DC: "To the extent there is any silver lining in this movement that we are seeing around the country, is the fact that we are openly having the conversation," Bottoms said. "Because there are so many biases that people have that they don't recognize they have. And it's not just with our police officers" (LaBlanc, 2020).

As reported by William Lee in the *Chicago Tribune*, Chris Fletcher a long-time veteran of the Chicago Police Department and the current chief of the Calumet City, Illinois Police Department said, "If you just looked at the media, you would think that the biggest issue for black folks is police brutality. But if you took a bloody weekend, all you've got to do is look at the number of people shot by police and the number of black people shot by black folks, and the (police) number pales in comparison" (Lee, 2016).

"IT AIN'T OVER TILL IT'S OVER" (as said by Yogi Berra)

We acknowledge how often whites and blacks when looking at the same picture observe two entirely different scenarios and messages. In spite of seeing differing reflections, what we say is neither about blackness nor whiteness, white racism nor black hatred. We are saying to focus on what is wrong and do what is right. Disrespect and a dangerous lifestyle are not attributes of any successful culture, but some pundits have no time to spend on the community unless it is spent on complaints and making profound statements. We are hoping pundits will take a breath and understand our purpose: to start a needed dialogue that has been stymied for too long.

I did not hear the word whitesplaining until early 2019, although I did understand its meaning. Whitesplaining is where a white person explains racism when, in fact, few white people really know what a black person experiences. Many talking heads in the media are guilty of whitesplaining. I have been guilty of saying black people see race in everything, although I have never said it to a black person. This thought is also one of a white man who has never walked in the shoes of a black man. I may be accused of whitesplaining when this book is published (Hein, personal communication, 2019).

I have never used the word whitesplaining and have only heard the word sparingly when discussing racial issues with people of color. In fact, I rarely discuss race with other black men. I have seen whitesplaining used more often in articles and newspapers. I am not comfortable with the word because of what it suggests: that a white person cannot have an opinion. Some discussion is better than none. With that said, there have been times when my white friends or colleagues have done or said something that I felt was racially insensitive. Many times I have ignored these incidents because I knew the person was unaware of their carelessness. I have always picked my battles and have often avoided a confrontation when I have considered an offense a minor issue because of the circumstances or the violator. I never felt that causing others to walk on eggshells would help to bridge the divide. There is a very good possibility I may not be considered "black enough" when this book is published (Franklin, personal communication, 2019).

Many instances of racism persist as members of white society dial 9–1–1 on members of black society who are perceived to be committing a criminal act when in fact the act is innocuous and not illegal. In addition, the death of black men, many of whom are unarmed, at the hands of police officers continue to ignite rage and anger in all Americans. As we conclude our efforts, we again recognized police improper use of force which apparently contributed to the death of George Floyd. Floyd's death was allegedly caused by a Minneapolis, Minnesota police officer who is clearly seen on video restraining Floyd with his knee against Floyd's neck. As Floyd is lying on the ground handcuffed, he is pleading with the officer that he cannot breathe. One can say the death of George Floyd is yet another striking event added to the pandemic of injustice, not only to the black community, but the entirety of society.

As we close our discussion of the contentious relationship between American law enforcement and black society, we understand there will be many skeptics of our beliefs. As we have discussed, in recent years various efforts have been made to improve police tactics. We believe American policing is changing but also understand it is changing too slowly; the system is still broken. We were amazed as most people were at the callous, unsympathetic treatment of George Floyd. Society, however, must realize the difficulty of changing the attitudes of some officers. Soon after of the death of George Floyd, the world saw some officers not maintaining order, not subduing violent protectors, but trying to defeat the protesters by attacking and assaulting them. A police officer maintains order during a demonstration by protecting themselves while controlling, dispersing and arresting people. An officer does not maintain order by driving vehicles into crowds or by pulling down a face mask to deliver pepper spray as seen on television. Likewise, one must also realize the difficulty of changing the attitudes, values, or spirit of some in society.

As more and more of these contentious confrontations occur, cross sections of society, comprised of both black and white citizens, finally debate how these types of incidents can be avoided. The problem we see is that debates and speeches are no longer enough. But political, religious, academic, and celebrity leaders among others who can make a sustained difference do not offer sufficient participation in making changes. We do, however, applaud rapper Killer Mike who made a passionate plea to violent protectors not to burn their own house down because of anger with an enemy. Unfortunately, we understand the enemy is the police. The rapper also said, "It is time to beat up prosecutors you don't like at the voting booth. . . . It is time to hold mayoral offices accountable, chiefs and deputy chiefs. . . . We want to see the system that sets up for systemic racism burned to the ground" (Croft, 2020). We can only wish rapper Killer Mike could have gone further than to save buildings and rightly criticize the establishment but also rallied to save the subculture of which we speak.

As the discussion continues, we wonder if society focused on the problems of the black subculture we have explored here, whether improvements would better the lives of all blacks. The introduction into mainstream society of those who may be undereducated, criminal or have violent tendencies, could lessen the apprehension of many. Remember many in white society, including police officers, fear the black antisocial subculture which apparently, in the minds of many, conveys to all blacks.

History is replete with celebrations of society's successes. It is less evident society avoids its failures. A continuation of failure with little to no effort to make corrections is a manifest error. As we write this, we see on television police officers joining peaceful protesters demonstrating against the death of George Floyd along with black and white citizens being interviewed calling for peace and unity among various cultures. It seems leadership, whether black or white, however lacking, is being overshadowed by social media and crowdsourcing. Absent leadership, many nondescript citizens are completing the task, but let us not forget the new-age mayors.

Still, the attitudes of police and citizens must change. Police must be associated with good, not bad. In response, citizens who lack social justice must accept social justice and show respect to others. We advocate but acknowledge this is a most difficult and uncomfortable conversation.

Whether white or black, red or brown or yellow, we believe society must help people who cannot help themselves. There will always be a segment of any community that for various reasons cannot, will not, or does not know how to help themselves. As we have stated, there are some in any subculture who lack the determination, the stamina, the resolve, or mentorship to enjoy a fruitful life. We are not racist for saying what we have said. We have exposed wrongs that need to be righted. Boys and girls, young men and women of all communities need protection until they can protect themselves. We say what we say because those who should have, did not. We offer no apology.

REFERENCES

Angelou, M. (1993). *Wouldn't take nothing for my journey now.* New York: Random House.

Croft, J. (2020). Killer Mike urges Atlanta protestors 'not to burn your own house down' in emotional plea. *CNN.* https://www.cnn.com/2020/05/30/us/killer-mike-atlanta-protest-rapper-trnd/index.html

Goodreads. (2019). *Notorious RBG quotes.* https://www.goodreads.com/work/quotes/44611586-notorious-rbg-the-life-and-times-of-ruth-bader-ginsburg

Held, A. (2018). 'Baby, It's Cold Outside,' seen as sexist, frozen out by radio stations. *National Public Radio.* https://www.npr.org/2018/12/05/673770902/baby-it-s-cold-outside-seen-as-sexist-frozen-out-by-radio-stations

LaBlanc, Paul. (2020). Atlanta major vows 'we will get to the other side of this' after latest police involved shooting. *CNN Politics.* https://www.cnn.com/2020/06/14/politics/keisha-lance-bottoms-mayors-who-matter-cnntv/index.html

Lee, W. (2016). For African-American police officers, a foot in two worlds. *Chicago Tribune.* https://www.chicagotribune.com/news/ct-african-american-officers-talk-about-crime-police-shootings-20160809-story.html

Levine, J. (2018). RoseAnne 'disgusted' by James Gunn defenders: 'the same people supported blacklisting me.' *The Wrap.* https://www.thewrap.com/roseanne-disgusted-by-james-gunn-supporters-blasts-double-standard/

Li, D., K., Fitzpatrick, S., & Fieldstadt, E. (2019). R. Kelly, charged with sexually abusing underage victims, has turned himself in. *NBC News.* https://www.nbcnews.com/news/us-news/r-kelly-charged-multiple-counts-sexual-abuse-minor-n974621

Nelson, E., & Furst, R. (2019). Five St. Paul police officers fired for failing to intervene in assault by ex-cop. *StarTribune.* http://www.startribune.com/five-st-paul-police-officers-fired-for-failing-to-intervene-in-assault/511254182/?refresh=true

Riddell, D. (2020). The billion-dollar move that Michael Jordan almost missed. *CNN Sports.* https://www.cnn.com/2020/05/03/sport/michael-jordan-billion-deal-almost-missed-cmd-spt-intl/index.html

Shoard, C. (2019). Kevin Hart rules himself out of Oscars hosting return. *The Guardian.* https://www.theguardian.com/film/2019/jan/10/kevin-hart-not-returning-to-host-oscars

Tan, G., & Porzecanski, K. (2018). Wall Street rules for the #MeTooEra: avoid women at all cost. *Bloomberg Business.* https://www.bloomberg.com/news/articles/2018-12-03/a-wall-street-rule-for-the-metoo-era-avoid-women-at-all-cost

Tara, J. (2018). PETA says phrases like 'bring home the bacon' are comparable to racism and homophobia. *CNN Cable News Network.* https://www.cnn.com/2018/12/05/europe/peta-meat-idioms-scli-intl/index.html

BIBLIOGRAPHY

ABC Action News. (2018). $105,000 taken in armored car heist outside bank in Tacony. Philadelphia, PA. http://6abc.com/news/heist-investigation-leads-to-roxborough apartment/29627/

Al Jazeera Media Network. (2017). Philando Castile killings: Police video sparks outrage. http://www.aljazeera.com/news/2017/06/philando-castile-killing-police-video-sparks-outrage-170621051241173.html

Alter, C. (2018). The young and the relentless: adults have failed to stop school shootings. Now it's the kids' turn to try. *TIME* [online]. Scribd, Inc. New York, NY. https://www.scribd.com/article/374705530/The-Young-And-The-Relentless

American Police Beat. (2019). *Judge oks "needed reforms" for Chicago Police Department.* Los Angeles, CA, *xxxvi*(3), 1, 21.

American Psychological Association. (n.d.). Socioeconomic status. https://www.apa.org/topics/socioeconomic-status/index

Angelou, M. (1993). *Wouldn't take nothing for my journey now.* New York: Random House.

Associated Press. (2017). A list of police ambush killings in the U.S., its territories. *Fox News.* https://www.foxnews.com/us/a-list-of-police-ambush-killings-in-the-us-its-territories

Association of State Criminal Investigative Agencies et al. (2017). National consensus policy and discussion paper on the use of force. https://www.theiacp.org/resources/document/national-consensus-discussion-paperon-use-of-force-and-consensus-policy

Athens, Lonnie H. (1992). *The creation of dangerous violent criminals.* Urbana and Chicago: University of Illinois Press.

Baker, A., Goodman, D.J., & Mueller, B. (2015). Beyond the chokehold: The path to Eric Garner's death. *The New York Times.* https://www.nytimes.com/2015/06/14/nyregion/eric-garner-police-chokehold- staten-island.html

Balko, R. (2012). Pentagon suspends program that gives military weapons to cops. *HuffPost.* https://www.huffpost.com/entry/pentagon-suspends-weapons-program-cops-military_n_1585328

Balko, R. (2013). *Rise of the warrior cop.* New York, NY: Public Affairs/Perseus Books Group, p. xii.

Balko, R. (2015). The increasing isolation of America's police. *The Washington Post.* https://www.washingtonpost.com/news/the-watch/wp/2015/05/11/the-increasing-isolation-of-americas-police/ ?utm_term=.37f5cca6ee80

Baltimore Sun, The. (2015). Police won't miss grenade launchers. Editorial. https: //www.baltimoresun.com/opinion/editorial/bs-ed-military-20150519story.html

Bauder, D. (2020). CBS News head calls threats against Gayle King reprehensible. *AP News.* https://apnews.com/1b8a3ad60aa2728fa721fb69e4af4b63

Beckett, Lois. (2014). *Black America's invisible crisis.* ESSENSE/ProPublica. https: //www.essence.com/news/propublica-post-traumatic-stress-disorder/

Bergland, C. (2013). Cortisol: why the "stress hormone" is public enemy no. 1. *Psychology Today.* https://www.psychologytoday.com/us/blog/the-athletes way /201301/cortisol-why-the-stress-hormone-is-public-enemy-no-1

Biography.com. (n.d.). Hammurabi. https://www.biography.com/people/hammura-bi-9327033

Black Lives Matter. (2017). What we believe. https://blacklivesmatter.com/about /what-we-believe/

Bloom, M. (2005). *Dying to kill: The allure of suicide terrorism.* New York, NY: Columbia University Press, pp. 5–6

Board of Trustees, University of Illinois. (2017). *Building the black metropolis: African American entrepreneurship in Chicago.* Robert E. Weems, Jr. & Jason P. Chambers (Eds.). Urbana: University of Illinois Press.

Brownson, J. (2017). Can't we all just get along? *Huff Post.* The Blog.

Bunn, C. (2020). Black health experts say surgeon general's comments reflect lack of awareness of black community. *NBC News.* https://www.nbcnews.com/news /nbcblk/black-health-experts-say-surgeon-general-s-comments-reflect-lack -n1183711

Burke, M. (2017). Dentist who fatally ran over husband after learning about his affairs granted parole. *The New York Daily News.*

Canterbury, C. (2016). Statement of Fraternal Order of Police national president Chuck Canterbury on recent violence against law enforcement officers. *Fraternal Order of Police.* https://fop.net/CmsDocument/Doc/pr_2016-1121.pdf

CBS News. (2017). Charlottesville protest report finds police failed at violent rally. https://www.cbsnews.com/news/charlottesville-protest-report-police-failed -violent-rally/#

CBS News. (2018). *Senate passes bipartisan criminal justice bill.* https://www .cbsnews.com/news/senate-passes-bipartisan-criminal- justice-bill-first-step-act -today-2018-12-18/

Center on Budget and Policy Priorities. (2017). Policy basics: Where do our federal tax dollars go? Washington, DC. https://www.cbpp.org/research/federal-budget /policy-basics-where-do-our-federal-tax-dollars-go

Charles, J. B. (2017). Justice Department ends era of pushing police reform. governing: the states and localities. https://www.governing.com/topics/public-justice -safety/lc-sessions-justice-police reforms-trump-doj-milwaukee.html

Cherry, K. (2018). Uninvolved parenting: characteristics, effects, and causes. *verywellmind.* https://www.verywellmind.com/what-is-uninvolved-parenting-2794958

Chicago Police Department. (2017). General order 03-02, use of force, summary of. Chicago Police Department. https://home.chicagopolice.org/use-of-force-policy/

Chicago Police Department. (2018). A better CPD for everyone. https://home .chicagopolice.org/office-of-reform-management/

City of Wilton Manors, Florida. (n.d). Auto burglary is a crime of opportunity. Auto-mobile Burglary Prevention Tips. https://www.wiltonmanors.com/301/Auto -Burglaries

Clark, M. (2014). Understanding Graham v. Connor. *Police: The Law Enforcement Magazine.* https://www.policemag.com/341717/understanding-graham-v-connor

CNN Library. (2017). Trayvon Martin shooting fast facts. *CNN News.* http://www .cnn.com/2013/06/05/us/trayvon-martin-shooting-fast-facts/index.html

Coalition of 11 American Law Enforcement Leadership and Union Organizations. (2017). National consensus policy and discussion paper on the use of force. https://www.theiacp.org/resources/document/national-consensus-discussion -paper-on-use-of-force-and-consensus-policy

Cole, N. L. (2017). *Why inner city youth suffer PTSD: Structural inequalities of race and class produce poor health outcomes.* ThoughtCo./Dotdash Publishing. https://www .thoughtco.com/hood-disease-is-a-racist-myth-3026666

College of Mount Saint Vincent. (2016). *Society of the individual: root causes of poverty in America.* Fishlinger Center for Public Policy Research. https://mountsaintvincent .edu/society-or-the-individual-root-causes-of-poverty-in america/

Comey, J. (2018). *A higher loyalty: truth, lies, and leadership.* New York, NY: Flatiron Books, pp. xi, 141–142.

Committee to Investigate Russia. (2017). How Russia operates. https://investigaterussia .org/how-russia-operates

Crain, C. (2020). What a white-supremacist coup looks like. *The New Yorker,* Books Issue. pp. 2, 5, 9. https://www.newyorker.com/magazine/2020/04/27/what-a -white-supremacist-coup-looks-like

Crepeau, M., Hinkel, D., Meisner, J., & Gorner, J. (2017). Three Chicago cops indict-ed in alleged cover-up of Laquan McDonald shooting details. *Chicago Tribune.* http://www.cnn.com/2017/06/27/us/chicago-officers-indicted-laquan-mcdonald /index.html

Crocq, M-A. & Crocq, L. (2000). *From shell shock to war neurosis to Posttraumatic Stress Disorder: A history of psychotraumatology. Dialogues Clin Neurosci, 2*(1), 47–55.

Croft, J. (2020). Killer Mike urges Atlanta protestors 'not to burn your own house down' in emotional plea. *CNN.* https://www.cnn.com/2020/05/30/us/killer -mike-atlanta-protest-rapper-trnd/index.html

Da Silva, C. (2018). NYPD will launch implicit bias training for police officers three years after Eric Garner's death. Newsweek. http://www.newsweek.com/nypd -start-implicit-bias-training-three-years-after-eric-garners-death-790248

Davey, M., & Bosman, J. (2014). Protests flair after Ferguson police officer is not in-dicted. *The New York Times.* https://www.nytimes.com/2014/11/25/us/ferguson -darren-wilson-shooting-michael-brown-grand-jury.html#

Davis, Merisa Parson. (2010). *Bill Cosby is right: but what should the church be doing about it?* www.xulonpress.com

Dees, T. (2014). *Why are there so many American local law enforcement characterizations and how do they all work together?* Quora. https://www.quora.com/Why-are-there -so-many-American-local-law-enforcement-characterizations-and-how-do-they -all-work-together

Diangelo, Robin. (2018). *White fragility: Why it's so hard for white people to talk about racism.* Boston, MA: Beacon Press.

Digital Library of Georgia. (2013). Civil Rights Digital Library. *Watts riots.* http://crdl.usg.edu/events/watts_riots/?Welcome

Donaghue, E. (2019). Cincinnati mayor pushes for bias training after two officers use racial slurs during calls. *CBS News.* https://www.cbsnews.com/news/cincinnati-mayor-john-cranley-pushes-for-bias-training-after-two-officers-use-racial-slurs-during-calls/

Dyson, M. E. (2005). *Is Bill Cosby right? or has the black middle class lost its mind?* New York, NY: Basic Civitas Books.

Eder, S., Protess, B., & Dewan S. (2017). How Trump's hands-off approach to policing is frustrating some chiefs. *The New York Times.* https://www.nytimes.com/2017/11/21/us/trump-justice-department-police.html

Eisenbaum, J. & Cooper, N. (2015). *Motive revealed in deadly shooting of Deputy Darren Goforth.* Click2Houston.com. https://www.click2houston.com/news/motive-revealed-in-deadly-shooting-of-deputy-darren-goforth

Ekins, E. (2017). *The state of free speech and tolerance in America. Survey Report.* Washington, DC: Cato Institute. https://www.cato.org/survey-reports/state-free-speech-tolerance-america

Engle, R., Benyon-Tinker, K., & Warner, K. (2019). Russian documents reveal desire to sow racial discord—and violence—in the US. *NBC News.* https://www.nbcnews.com/news/world/russian-documents-reveal-desire-sow-racial-discord-violence-u-s-n1008051

Eversley, M, Lackey, K. & Hughes, T. (2014). 2 NYPD officers killed in ambush-style shooting. *USA Today.* https://www.usatoday.com/story/news/nation/2014/12/20/new-york-city-police-officers-shot/20698679/

Federal Bureau of Investigation. (2016). *Uniform Crime Report.* https://ucr.fbi.gov/crime-in-the.u.s/2016/crime-in-the-u.s.-2016/topic-pages/violent crime

Federal Bureau of Investigation. (2018). *What We Investigate: Terrorism.* https://www.fbi.gov/investigate/terrorism

Federal Bureau of Investigation. (n.d). Services. *National Academy.* https://www.fbi.gov/services/training-academy/national-academy

Ford, M. (2017). A major victory for the right to record police. *The Atlantic.* https://www.theatlantic.com/politics/archive/2017/07/a-major-victory-for-the-right-to-record-police/533031/

Fortin, J. (2017). Iowa man is sentenced to 2 life terms in killings of 2 officers. *The New York Times.* https://www.nytimes.com/2017/05/19/us/scott-michael-greene-iowa.html

Fraternal Order of Police. (n.d.). *A history of the Fraternal Order of Police.* https://www.fop.net/CmsPage.aspx?id=13

Florida National University. (2018). *What did Martin Luther King, Jr. accomplish for minorities.* https://www.fnu.edu/martin-luther-king-jr-accomplished-minorities/

Fortin, J., & Bromwich, J. E. (2017). Cleveland police officer who shot Tamir Rice is fired. *The New York Times.* https://www.nytimes.com/2017/05/30/us/cleveland-police-tamir-rice.html

Fox News Entertainment and the Associated Press. (2015). NYPD union calls for boycott Quentin Tarantino films after director's anti-cop protest. http://www .foxnews.com/entertainment/2015/10/26/nypd-calls-for-boycott-quentin-tarantino -after-director-leads-anti-cop-protest.html

Gaouetter, N., Cohen, M., & Conte, M. (2020). Putin leverages coronavirus chaos to make a direct play to Trump. *CNN News.* https://www.cnn.com/2020/04/18 /politics/trump-putin-unprecedented-contacts/index.html

Garrick, D. (2017). San Diego boosts police pay up to 30 percent amid staffing crisis. *The San Diego Union-Tribune.* http://www.sandiegouniontribune.com/news /politics/sd-me-police-raises-20171205-story.html

Geary, D. (2015). Moynihan report: an annotated edition. a historian unpacks the Negro family: the case for national action on its 50th anniversary. *The Atlantic.* https://www.theatlantic.com/politics/archive/2015/09/the-moynihan-report -anannotated edition/404632/

Gibson, C. (2016). What happened in Chicago in 1968, and why is everyone talking about it now? *The Washington Post.* https://www.washingtonpost.com/news /arts-and-entertainment/wp/2016/07/18/what-happened-in-chicago-in-1968 -and-why-is-everyone-talking-about-it-now/?utm_term=.9008e6100063

Goldman, A. (2017). Trump reverses restrictions on military hardware for police. *The New York Times.* https://www.nytimes.com/2017/08/28/us/politics/trump -police-military-surplus-equipment.html

Goldman, A., Barnes, J., Haberman, M. & Fandos, N. (2020). Lawmakers are warned that Russia is meddling to re-elect Trump. *The New York Times.* https: //www.nytimes.com/2020/02/20/us/politics/russian-interference-trump -democrats.html

Goodreads. (2019). *Notorious RBG quotes.* https://www.goodreads.com/work/quotes /44611586-notorious-rbg-the-life-and-times-of-ruth-bader-ginsburg

Gorner, J., Nickeas, P., Malagon, E., & Chachkevitch, A. (2016). Chicago top cop: It's society, not police. *Chicago Tribune.* https://www.policeone.com/Officer -Safety/ articles/218799006-Chicago-top-cop-Its-/

Graham, D. A. (2017). The murder of Miosotis Familia. *The Atlantic Daily.* https://www.theatlantic.com/news/archive/2017/07/the-murder-of-miosotis -familia/532707/

Griggs, B. (2018). Living while black: here are all the routine activities for which police were called on African-Americans this year. *Cable News Network.* https: //www.cnn.com/2018/12/20/us/living-while-black-police-calls-trnd/index.html

Grossman, Dave. Lt. Col. (2007). *On combat: The psychology and physiology of deadly conflict in war and peace.* Warrior Science Publications.

Grunlund, M. (2017). Abner Luoima: 20 years since infamous attach by ex-cop Justin Volpe. *Staten Island Real-Time News. Silive.com.* http://www.npr.org/2017 /04/26/524744989/when-la-erupted-in-anger-a-look-back-at-the-rodney-king -riots

Guardian, The. (2015). Tulsa officer who fatally shot Eric Harris 'regrets' using gun instead of Taser. *The Guardian.* https://www.theguardian.com/us-news/2015 /apr/17/tulsa-oklahoma-police-shooting-robert-bates-eric-harris-apology

Hajela, D. (2018). Sympathy for white Austin bomber stirs debate about race. *PBS News Hour.* https://www.pbs.org/newshour/nation/sympathy-for-white-austin -bomber-stirs-debate-about-race

Hallman, T. & Rajwani, N. (2018). Dallas Police Department hiring lags as firefighting hiring surges. Dallas, TX: *The Dallas Morning News.* https://www.dallasnews .com/news/dallas-city-hall/2018/01/29/dallas-police-department-hiring-lags -firefighter-hiring-surges

Haskins, R. (2009). *The sequence of personal responsibility.* Washington, DC: The Brookings Institution. https://www.brookings.edu/articles/the-sequence-of-personal -responsibility/

Hein, J. F. (1980). *Education: A way of changing the police image.* University Park, IL: Governor's State University, pp. 174-175.

Hein, J. F. 2013. *Inside internal affairs: An in-depth look at the people, process & politics.* Flushing, NY: Looseleaf Law Publications, pp. 16, 64, 205.

Held, A. (2018). 'Baby, It's Cold Outside,' seen as sexist, frozen out by radio stations. *National Public Radio.* https://www.npr.org/2018/12/05/673770902/baby-it-s -cold-outside-seen-as-sexist-frozen-out-by-radio-stations

Howard, Philip K. (1994). *Death of common sense, the: How law is suffocating America.* New York: Random House.

Ingersoll, S. (2019). Judge goes on tirade about black-on-black crime, saying it puts klan to shame. *Clarksville Leaf-Chronicle.* https://www.theleafchronicle.com /story/news/local/clarksville/2019/01/04/tennessee-judge-tirade-black-crime -wayne-shelton/2482403002/

Jackman, T. (2017). Do federal consent decrees improve local police departments? This study says they might. *The Washington Post.* https://www.washingtonpost .com/news/true-crime/wp/2017/05/24/__trashed/

Jeffries, M. P., (2014). Ferguson must force us to face anti-blackness. *Boston Globe.* https://www.bostonglobe.com/opinion/2014/11/28/ferguson-must-force-face -anti-blackness/pKVMpGxwUYpMDyHRWPln2M/story.html

Johnson, A. (2016). Tulsa reserve deputy convicted of manslaughter in death of Eric Harris. *NBC News.* https://www.nbcnews.com/news/us-news/tulsa-reserve -deputy-convicted-manslaughter-death-eric-harris-n563836

Johnson, H. (2008). 1968 Democratic Convention: the bosses strike back. *Smithsonian Magazine.* Smithsonian.com. https://www.smithsonianmag.com/history /1968-democratic-convention-931079/

Johnson, K. (2017). Should cops be able to fire warning shots in tense situations? even police sharply disagree. *USA Today.* https://www.usatoday.com/story/news /politics/2017/10/25/new-policy-allows-police-use-warning-shots-cops-disagree -new-policy-allowing-police-use-warning-shot/798338001/

Johnson, L, B. (1964). *January 8, 1964: State of the Union.* Miller Center. University of Virginia. https://millercenter.org/the-presidency/presidential-speeches/january -8-1964-state-union

Kappeler, V. E., Ph.D. (2014). A brief history of slavery and the origins of American policing. *Eastern Kentucky University police studies online,* p. 1. http://plsonline.eku .edu/insidelook/brief-history-slavery-and-origins-american-policing

Kendi, Ibram, X. (2017). *Stamped from the beginning: the definitive history of racist ideas in America.* New York, NY: Bold Type Books.

Kertscher, T. (2017). Do 90% of Americans support background checks for all gun sales? *Politifact/Wisconsin in partnership with the Journal Sentinel.* http://www .politifact.com/wisconsin/statements/2017/oct/03/chris-abele/do-90-americans -support-background-checks-all-gun-/

Khan-Cullour, Patrisse & Bandele, Asha. (2017). *When they call you a terrorist: A Black Lives Matter memoir.* New York, NY: St. Martin's Press.

Klein, J. (2014). History of police unions. *Encyclopedia of Criminology and Criminal Justice,* pp. 2207–2217. https://doi.org/10.1007/978-1-4614-5690-2_463

Korte, G. (2015). Obama bans some military equipment sales to police. *USA TODAY.* https://www.usatoday.com/story/news/politics/2015/05/18/obama -police-military-equipment-sales-new-jersey/27521793/

Kozlowska, H. (2017). U.S. police forces are practicing mindfulness to reduce officers' stress—and violence. *Quartz Media, LLC.* https://qz.com/1025231/police -departments-in-the-us-are-practicing-mindfulness-to-reduce-officers-stress-and -violence/

Kusch, F. (2004). *Battleground Chicago: The police and the 1968 Democratic National Convention.* Chicago, IL: University of Chicago Press.

Kwanzaa Official Website. (2020). Nguzo Saba [Seven Principles of Kwanzaa]. http: //www.officialkwanzaawebsite.org/umoja.html

LaBlanc, Paul. (2020). Atlanta major vows 'we will get to the other side of this' after latest police involved shooting. *CNN Politics.* https://www.cnn.com/2020/06 /14/politics/keisha-lance-bottoms-mayors-who-matter-cnntv/index.html

LeVine, M. (2001). 9/11: one year later. 10 Things to Know About Terrorism. *Alternet.org.* https://www.alternet.org/story/11647/10_things_to_know_about _terrorism

Law.com (2020). *Parental neglect.* https://dictionary.law.com/Default.aspx?selected =1446

Lee, W. (2016). For African-American police officers, a foot in two worlds. *Chicago Tribune.* https://www.chicagotribune.com/news/ct-african-american-officers-talk -about-crime-police-shootings-20160809-story.html

Levine, J. (2018). RoseAnne 'disgusted' by James Gunn defenders: 'the same people supported blacklisting me.' *The Wrap.* https://www.thewrap.com/roseanne -disgusted-by-james-gunn-supporters-blasts-double-standard/

Li, D., K., Fitzpatrick, S., & Fieldstadt, E. (2019). R. Kelly, charged with sexually abusing underage victims, has turned himself in. *NBC News.* https://www.nbc news.com/news/us-news/r-kelly-charged-multiple-counts-sexual-abuse-minor -n974621

Liang, Q., & Wang X. (1999). *Unrestricted warfare: China's master plan to destroy America.* Beijing, China: PLA Literature and Arts Publishing House.

Litten, K. (2017). Read the suicide note left by Baton Rouge police shooter Gavin Long. New Orleans, LA: *The Times-Picayune.* http://www.nola.com/politics /index.ssf/2017/06/baton_rouge_police_shooting_2.html

Love, D, A. (2018). Russia's targeting of black voters is a very American thing to do. *Cable News Network*. https://www.cnn.com/2018/12/19/opinions/senate-reports -russia-facebook-2016-election-and-race-david-love/index.html

Makary, M. (2012). *Unaccountable: what hospitals wont't tell you and how transparency can revolutionize health care.* New York, NY: Bloomsbury Press, pp. 17–57.

Mannix, A. (2019). Minneapolis to ban 'warrior' training for police Mayor Jacob Frey says. *Star Tribune*. http://www.startribune.com/minneapolis-to-ban-warrior -training-for-police/508756392/

Martine, G. E. (2016). Six ways president Obama reformed American Criminal Justice System. *NewsOne*. https://newsone.com/3590472/president-obama-criminal -justice-reform/

Marrero, T. (2016). Tampa police union supports boycott of Beyoncé's music but doesn't tell members not to work her Tampa concert. *Tampa Bay Times*. http: //www.tampabay.com/news/publicsafety/will-tampa-police-officers-heed-call-to -boycott-beyonces-concert/2265915

Matthews, D. (2012). Poverty in the 50 years since 'the other America,' in five charts. *The Washington Post*. https://www.washingtonpost.com/news/wonk/wp/2012 /07/11/poverty-in-the-50-years-since-the-other-america-in-five-charts/?utm_term =.a72b80a47da3

Mayo Clinic, Patient Care and Health Information. (2019). *Post-traumatic stress disor-der.* Mayo Foundation for Medical Education and Research. https://www.mayo clinic.org/diseases-conditions/post-traumatic-stress-disorder/symptoms-causes /syc-20355967

McKew, M, K. (2017). The Gerasimov Doctrine: it's Russia's new chaos theory of political warfare. And it's probably being used on you. *Politico Magazine*. https: //www.politico.com/magazine/story/2017/09/05/gerasimov-doctrine-russia-for eign- policy-215538

McDonell-Parry, A., & Barron, J. (2017). Death of Freddie Gray: 5 things you didn't know. *Rolling Stone*. http://www.rollingstone.com/culture/features/death-of -freddie-gray-5-things-you-didnt-know-w476107

Melley, B. (2016). Law enforcement condemns letters threatening Muslims. *Asso-ciated Press*. https://www.policeone.com/federal-law-enforcement/articles /244530006-Law-enforcement-condemns-letters-threatening-Muslims/ ?NewsletterID=244211044&utm_source=iContact&utm_medium=email&utm _content=TopNewsRight1Title&utm_campaign=P1Member&cub_id=usr_W5 W3xYBArFqaU1OQ

Meyerson, C. (2016). 5 Milestone accomplishments from the year in Black Lives Matter. *Gizmodo Media Group, Splinter News*. https://splinternews.com/5-mile stone-accomplishments-from-the-year-in-black-live-1793864356

Moodie-Mills, D. (2017). The 'Green Book' was a travel guide just for black motorists. *NBC News*. https://www.nbcnews.com/news/nbcblk/green-book-was -travel-guide-just-black-motorists-n649081

Mosendz, P. (2015). Chicago officials release video of white police officer shooting black teenager. *Newsweek*. http://www.newsweek.com/chicago-police-officer -charged-murder-black-teenager-398031

Move for Black Lives. (n.d.). Platform. https://policy.m4bl.org/platform/

National Public Radio. (2017). When L.A. erupted in anger: a look back at the Rodney King riots. http://www.npr.org/2017/04/26/524744989/when-la-erupted -in-anger-a-look-back-at-the-rodney-king-riots

Nelson, E., & Furst, R. (2019). Five St. Paul police officers fired for failing to intervene in assault by ex-cop. *StarTribune.* http://www.startribune.com/five-st-paul -police-officers-fired-for-failing-to-intervene-in-assault/511254182/?refresh=true

New York City Police Department. (2017). *2017 use of force report.* https://www1 .nyc.gov/assets/nypd/downloads/pdf/use-of-force/use-of-force-2017.pdf

New York City Police Department. (2018). *Neighborhood policing.* https://www1 .nyc.gov/site/nypd/bureaus/patrol/neighborhood-coordination- officers.page

New York Post. (2015). 5 police corruption scandals that rocked New York City. *New York Post.* https://nypost.com/dispatch/5-police-corruption-scandals-that-rocked -new-york-city/

New York Times, The. (2015). What happened in Ferguson? *The New York Times.* https://www.nytimes.com/interactive/2014/08/13/us/ferguson-missouri-town -under-siege-after-police-shooting.html

Nunnelly, W.A. (1991). *Bull Connor.* Tuscaloosa, AL: University of Alabama Press, p. 162.

Obama, B. (2017). The president's role in advancing criminal justice reform: The urgent need for reform. *Harvard Law Review, 30*(3). https://harvardlawreview .org/2017/01/the-presidents-role-in-advancing-criminal-justice-reform/

Olsen, T. (2017). Duluth police recruits will test 'customer service' training. *Duluth News Tribune.* https://www.policeone.com/police-training/articles/461444006 -Minn-police-department-to-provide-customer-service-training-to-new-recruits/

Parker, D. (2015). Recent slayings of unarmed black men showcase culture of police violence. *American Civil Liberties Union.* https://www.aclu.org/blog/racial-justice /race-and-criminal-justice/recent-slayings-unarmed-black-men-showcase-culture

Patients and Families. (2018). What is Posttraumatic Stress Disorder? *American Psychiatric Association.* https://www.psychiatry.org/patients-families/ptsd/what-is -ptsd

Perkins, J. M. (2017). *Dream with me: race, love, and the struggle we must win.* Grand Rapids, MI: Baker Books.

Pilgram, D., Ph.D. (2012). *The garbage man: Why I collect racist objects.* Farris State University, Jim Crow Museum of Racist Memorabilia, https://www.ferris.edu /HTMLS/news/jimcrow/collect.htm

President's Task Force on 21st Century Policing. (2015). *Final report of president's task force on 21st century policing.* Washington, DC: Office of Community Oriented Policing Services. https://cops.usdoj.gov/pdf/taskforce/taskforce_finalreport .pdf

Psychology Today. (n.d.). What is groupthink? Sussex Publishers, LLC. https://www .psychologytoday.com/basics/groupthink

Psychology Today. (2018). What is mindfulness? Sussex Publishers, Inc. https: //www.psychologytoday.com/us/basics/mindfulness

Regis University. School of Contemporary Liberal Studies. (2016). *What causes some-one to exhibit criminal behavior?* Denver, CO. https://primusaplang.wordpress.com /2017/09/27/what-causes-someone-to-exhibit-criminal-behavior-regis-criminology -programs-17-mar-2016-criminology-regis-educriminology-programsresource scrim-articleswhat-causes-someone-to/

Reuters. (2007). Chronology: who banned slavery when? https://www.reuters.com /article/uk-slavery/chronology-who-banned-slavery-when-idUSL15614649 20070322

Riddell, D. (2020). The billion-dollar move that Michael Jordan almost missed. *CNN Sports.* https://www.cnn.com/2020/05/03/sport/michael-jordan-billion-deal -almost-missed-cmd-spt-intl/index.html

Roberts, Paul, C. & Stratton, Lawrence, M. (1995). *The new color line: how quotas and privilege destroy democracy.* Washington, DC: Regnery Publishing, Inc.

Robinson, P. H. & Robinson, S. M. (2015). *Pirates, prisoners, & lepers: Lessons from life outside the law.* Potomac Books. The University of Nebraska Press

Ross, J. (2016). Two decades later, black and white Americans finally agree on O.J. Simpson's guilt. *The Washington Post.* https://www.washingtonpost.com/news /the-fix/wp/2015/09/25/black-and-white-americans-can-now-agree-o-j-was -guilty/?utm_term=.ad5deb90e64b

Rush, G. E. (2000). Consent decree. *The Dictionary of Criminal Justice* (5th ed.). Dushkin/McGraw Hill.

Sewer, A. (2015). Bill Cosby's famous "pound cake" speech, annotated. *BuzzFeed News.* https://www.buzzfeednews.com/article/adamserwer/bill-cosby-pound-for-pound

Shoard, C. (2019). Kevin Hart rules himself out of Oscars hosting return. *The Guardian.* https://www.theguardian.com/film/2019/jan/10/kevin-hart-not -returning-to-host-oscars

Shults, J. F. (2014). How outdated police media strategy lost the Twitter-verse in Ferguson. *PoliceOne.com.* https://www.policeone.com/social-media-for-cops /articles/7479178-How-outdated-police-media-strategy-lost-the-Twitter-verse-in -Ferguson/

Sisario, B. & Sperling, N. (2020). Pressure by Simmons over expose', Oprah Winfrey faced a big decision. *The New York Times.* https://www.nytimes.com/2020/01/17 /movies/oprah-winfrey-russell-simmons-movie.html

Smith, Ronald L. (1997). *Cosby: The life of a comedy legend.* Buffalo, NY: Prometheus Books.

Spanos, B. (2016). Beyoncé explains why 'formation' video is not anti-police. *Rolling Stone.* http://www.rollingstone.com/music/news/beyonce-businesswoman-role -burden-and-blessing-20160405

Spector, Elliot, B. (2017). *Beyond black lives matter.* Flushing, NY: Looseleaf Law Publications, Inc.

Spielman, F. (2015). Disgraced Chicago cop Jon Burge breaks silence, condemns $5.5 million reparations fund. *Chicago Sun-Times.* https://chicago.suntimes.com /2015/4/17/18469974/disgraced-chicago-cop-jon-burge-breaks-silence-condemns -5-5-million-reparations-fund

Stamper, N. (2005). *Breaking rank: A top cop's expose' of the dark side of American policing.* New York, NY: Nation Books.

Stamper, N. (2016). *To protect and serve: How to fix America's police.* New York, NY: Nations Books, p. xviii.

Stinson, P. M., Liederbach, J., Lab, S. P., & Brewer, S. L. (2016). *Police integrity lost: A study of law enforcement officers arrested. final technical report.* Institute of Justice, Office of Justice Programs, U.S. Department of Justice, pp. 15, 21/22, 189/192. https://www.ncjrs.gov/pdffiles1/nij/grants/249850.pdf

Surgeon General, Office of. National Center for Injury Prevention and Control. National Institute of Mental Health. Center for Mental Health Services. (2001). *Youth violence: A report of the Surgeon General.* Rockville, MD. https://www.ncbi.nlm.nih.gov/books/NBK44293/#A12607

Tan, G., & Porzecanski, K. (2018). Wall Street rules for the #MeTooEra: avoid women at all cost. *Bloomberg Business.* https://www.bloomberg.com/news/articles/2018-12-03/a-wall-street-rule-for-the-metoo-era-avoid-women-at-all-cost

Tara, J. (2018). PETA says phrases like 'bring home the bacon' are comparable to racism and homophobia. *CNN Cable News Network.* https://www.cnn.com/2018/12/05/europe/peta-meat-idioms-scli-intl/index.html

Tarm, M. (2018). Trump administration opposes Chicago police reform plan. *Associated Press.* https://www.apnews.com/36187d7582a84eb6b4b4e542985aba29

Tayler, G. Flint. (2012). A long and winding road: the struggle for justice in the Chicago police torture cases. People's Law Office. *Loyola Public Interest Reporter.* Loyola University, Chicago. http://peopleslawoffice.com/wp-content/uploads/2012/06/A-long-and-winding-road-for-justice-in-chicago-police-torture-civil-rights-cases.pdf

Thompson, K., & Wilson, S. (2012). Obama on Trayvon Martin: 'if I had a son, he'd look like Trayvon.' *The Washington Post.* https://www.washingtonpost.com/politics/obama-if-i-had-a-son-hed-look-like-trayvon/2012/03/23/gIQApKPpVS_story.html

Tunnell, H. (2014). *The Negro motorist green book (1936–1964).* BlackPast.org. Online Reference Guide to African American History. https://blackpast.org/aah/negro-motorist-green-book-1936-1964

University of California, Davis. (2017). Center for Poverty Research. *Current estimates of poverty in the U.S.* https://poverty.ucdavis.edu/faq/what-current-poverty-rate-united-states

USAonline. (2018). State and local governments. http://www.theusaonline.com/government/state-local-government.htm

U.S. Census Bureau. (2017). Income and Poverty in the United States: 2016. *People and family in poverty by selected characteristics: 2015 and 2016 [table 3].* https://www.census.gov/library/publications/2017/demo/p60-259.html

U.S. Department of Justice. (2017). Office of Community Oriented Policing Services. FY 2018. *Congressional justification.* https://www.justice.gov/file/969011/download

U.S. Department of Justice, Civil Rights Division and United States Attorney's Office Northern District of Illinois. (2017). *Investigation of the Chicago Police Department.* https://www.justice.gov/opa/file/925846/download

U.S. Department of Justice. (2018). Office of Community Oriented Policing Services. *Problem solving.* https://cops.usdoj.gov/problemsolving

Wadman, R. C., & Allison, W. T. (2004). *To protect and to serve: A history of police in America.* Pearson Education, 47–51, 67–81.

Walker, S. (1977). *A critical history of police reform: The emergence of professionalism.* Lexington, MA: D.C. Heath & Co., pp. 25-58.

Walsh, M. (2015). From 'I am a man' to "Black Lives Matter'. *OZY.com.* http://www.ozy.com/flashback/from-i-am-a-man-to-black-lives-matter/61443

Washington Post, The. (n.d.). *Fatal force. The Washington Post.* https://www.washingtonpost.com/graphics/national/police-shootings-2017/

Watson, K. (2018). Trump signs criminal justice reform bill. *CBS News.* https://www.cbsnews.com/news/trump-signs-criminal-justice-reform-bill-live-updates/?ftag=CNM-00-10aac3a

Waxman, O. B. (2016). Police group apologizes for law enforcement's history as "face of oppression." *TIME* [online] http://time.com/4535103/historical-mistreatment-police-chiefs-african-americans-speech/

White House, The, Office of the Press Secretary. (2015). *Executive order—federal support for local law enforcement equipment acquisition.* https://www.bja.gov/publications/LEEWG_Report_Final.pdf

Workneh, L. (2016). 11 big accomplishments black activists achieved in 2015. *HuffPost.* https://www.huffingtonpost.com/entry/11-big-accomplishments-black-activists-achieved-in-2015_us_567996bae4b0b958f6583320

Wright State University. (n.d.). *Code of Hammurabi. c. 1700 B.C.E.* Dayton, OH. http://www.wright.edu/~christopher.oldstone-moore/Hamm.htm

WSMV-TV News. (2017). Police arrest accused serial bank robber after Saturday robbery. Nashville, TN. https://www.wsmv.com/news/police-arrest-accused-serial-bank-robber-after-saturday-robbery/article_574deb40-8a16-5c9b-a292-47b6ad4f2bf5.html

WTTW Public Broadcasting digital archives. (2016). Power, politics, & pride: Afro-American Patrolmen's League. https://interactive.wttw.com/dusable-to-obama/afro-american-patrolmens-league

Wyllie, D. (2015). 3 crucial points about Obama's evisceration of the 1033 Program. *PoliceOne.com.* https://www.policeone.com/patrol-issues/articles/8550404-3-crucial-points-about-/

Yan, H., Khushbu, S., & Grinberg, E. (2017). Ex-officer Michael Slager pleads guilty to shooting death of Walter Scott. *Cable News Network.* http://www.cnn.com/2017/05/02/us/michael-slager-federal-plea/index.html

Yen, H. (2019). AP Fact Check. Trump exaggerates his role in black job gains. *AP News.* https://apnews.com/f78f4205f474482db8bb8fa7a5ebfa27

INDEX